"For the word of God is full of living power."

Hebrews 4:12

POWER
FOR LIVING

by
Jamie Buckingham

Commissioned by
the
Arthur S. DeMoss Foundation

Revised Edition
April 1999

Power For Living trademark is used by permission of Cook Communications Ministries.

Printed in the United States of America

1st edition published October 1983
2nd edition (revised), published November 1983
2nd edition, 2nd printing, September 1984
2nd edition (revised), 3rd printing, November 1984
2nd edition (revised), 4th printing, February 1985
3rd edition (revised), 5th printing, October 1998
4th edition (revised), 6th printing, November 1998
4th edition, 7th printing, January 1999
5th edition (revised), 8th printing, April 1999
5th edition, 9th printing, August 1999
5th edition, 10th printing, January 2000

ISBN 0-8423-1816-X

POWER FOR LIVING

CONTENTS

READ THIS FIRST

One Sunday morning, not too long ago, three men crawled into the cockpit of a strange looking spaceship which was strapped to a giant rocket at Cape Kennedy, Florida. As the entire free world watched in fascination, the countdown for spaceship *Columbia* began.

Never before had a spaceship taken off from earth, orbited the globe, and returned. It took an awful lot of power to make it happen.

The rocket itself was 184 feet tall.

It weighed four and one half million pounds.

It carried a half million gallons of fuel.

It generated five million pounds of thrust—enough power to push the spaceship to the altitude of 23 miles in two minutes.

After the initial take-off, *Columbia* climbed to the altitude of 189 miles and circled the globe at 17,000 miles per hour.

Altogether it made 113 orbits in seven days.

It was one of the greatest displays of power the world had ever seen.

Journalists compared the spaceship to an eagle. But it

wasn't an eagle. It was simply a big hunk of metal. And when it ran out of power it fell out of the sky, its belly glowing white-hot from reentry into the atmosphere, and finally glided to a stop on the salt flats in the desert of California.

Spaceship *Columbia* was a magnificent scientific feat. But its power to leave earth, indeed its momentum to stay aloft, was created by man.

Eagles, because of their ability to find the thermals—those columns of warm air which rise from the earth—are able to stay aloft indefinitely, often without even moving their great wings. But *Columbia* was not an eagle. It was a spaceship. As a result, it was destined to fall to earth.

The only way it could become an eagle was to be born an eagle—or be reborn as one.

That's the problem with most of us—with all of us. We have a certain amount of natural power. But for some reason, we don't have enough to make it all the way to the end. A few seem to get a good start, but even they fall to earth in the long run. And the rest of us never do even get off the launching pad. We just sit there and sputter. Sometimes we don't even have enough power to do that, and the first little breeze that comes along topples us into the dust where we lay forgotten—as though we never existed in the first place.

Recently a group of highly successful people, people who have risen to the top of their profession, were asked about their lives. These people are not hunks of metal, destined to come tumbling down sooner or later. They are like true eagles—soaring the heights. When they were asked about the power that keeps them aloft, they all gave the same answer.

God.

That's right, they said their power for living came from

a personal relationship with God. Unlike the spaceship *Columbia,* which was put aloft by man's efforts, they all said they had tried man's way and found it empty. But when they turned to God and allowed Him to take control of their lives, they began to soar.

"God?" you say. "Well, He might be able to help folks who already have made it. But what about me?"

Wait a minute. God is not just for the famous, or the rich, or those nice folks who dress up to go to church or the synagogue. God is for everyone. He loves those who are helpless. He loves the alcoholics, the drug addicts, those who have lost power and are tumbling end over end in space, headed for a sure crack-up (unless they burn out first on reentry). He loves the fellow who's out of work, the homemaker caught in the web of adultery, the lonely teenager, the frustrated businessman.

He loves you. And if you will let Him, He will not only direct your path, but will give you power to live.

That's what this book is all about. Power for living. A long time ago the prophet Isaiah discovered this. What he wrote has been tested by millions of people from all walks of life, across the years. Now it's your time to test it, too, and let God give you power, not only to live but to live abundantly. Here's what Isaiah said: ***"But those who wait on the Lord will find new strength. They will fly high on wings like eagles. They will run and not grow weary. They will walk and not faint"*** (Isaiah 40:31).

Jamie Buckingham
Melbourne, Florida

Seek His will in all you do,
and He will direct your paths.
Proverbs 3:6

REACHING YOUR GOAL

Everyone dreams of success. It is their goal, or destination, in life.

Some see success as making a lot of money, living comfortably, and retiring early.

Others dream of becoming proficient in their field, making money, and having folks look up to them as important and wise.

Still others see success as the accumulation of material things—without debt. Owning your own house, driving an expensive car, being able to walk into the store and buy anything you want. That's success.

Then there are those who equate success with having a happy family: a loving wife or husband and obedient children.

To others success is long life, free from disease and heartache.

Everyone has a dream of success.

The Bible says that if you *"take delight in the Lord . . . and He will give you your heart's desires"* (Psalms 37:4). That's a marvelous promise. The problem, it seems, is that it seldom happens. I mean, if it did, it seems many would be healthy, wealthy and wise—for that's what we desire, isn't it?

Why then aren't we successful—if that's the desire of our heart?

Could it be that we have a wrong idea of what success is? Is it possible we haven't listened to God's conditions for success?

The first condition listed—indeed, the only condition listed—is to "take delight in the Lord." In other words, put God first. Jesus said the same thing when He told His disciples that if they would *"live for Him and make the Kingdom of God [their] primary concern,"* everything else necessary for life would be given them as well (Matthew 6:33).

Our problem is not that we don't have goals. Our problem is having the wrong goals.

GETTING OFF AT THE WRONG PLACE

Last year I boarded a plane in New York to fly to my home in Melbourne, Florida. The plane made one stop en route at Tampa before flying on to Melbourne. Since we were running behind schedule, the flight attendant asked all the Melbourne passengers to remain on the plane during the brief stop in Tampa.

I was busy reading and didn't pay much attention to what was going on, but I began to realize we had been on the ground in Tampa much longer than usual. I asked one of the flight attendants what was wrong.

"We've lost two of our Melbourne passengers," she said. "They accidentally got off here in Tampa and we haven't been able to find them and get them back on the plane."

In a few minutes two elderly women came rushing aboard the plane. They were obviously flustered and speaking rapid Italian to each other, complete with hand gestures. The flight attendant got them buckled in, and we immediately took off for the short flight across the state to Melbourne.

After we were aloft, the flight attendant stopped by my seat and told me what had happened. The two women were from Italy. They spoke no English. This was their first trip to the United States. They were visiting family members who lived in the Melbourne area—and who were waiting for them at the Melbourne airport. It was the biggest trip of their lives and they were excited—and a little scared.

They had boarded in Rome for the long flight to the United States, then changed planes in New York for the flight south to Melbourne. Since they could not understand English, they did not realize the domestic flight made a stop in Tampa before flying on to Melbourne. When the plane landed in Tampa and they looked out the window and saw palm trees waving in the Florida sun, they assumed they had reached their destination. They joined the crowd getting off in Tampa and hurried off the plane looking for their loved ones who had promised to meet them at the airport.

What they failed to realize was that they were 120 miles short of the goal. They had gotten off in Tampa thinking their dream of a lifetime was at last fulfilled, only to discover they were lost in a huge airport with no loved ones to meet them.

The flight attendants finally found them wandering dazed through the strange terminal. But when they tried to convince them to get back on the plane, they refused. They mistakenly thought they were going to be sent back to their home country. Someone finally found a baggage handler who spoke Italian. He explained they were not where they were supposed to be. Only then did the women rush back on the plane, eager to go on to their final destination.

Most of us are like that. For some reason—maybe it's because we don't understand God's language in the Bible—we get off at the wrong destination. We equate money, security, and prestige with success. We don't understand that true success is found in having our spiritual needs met. Few of us ever arrive at that ultimate success because we are too busy rushing through the airport of material success.

What are the things that cause you to get off in Tampa when your real need is to go to Melbourne?

There could be a lot of reasons. Maybe you don't understand the language. What you need is an interpreter. Someone to come along and explain God's directions.

Or maybe someone gave you bad directions. There are a lot of folks wandering around who seem to delight in misleading people these days. That's one of the reasons we've given you this book—to help you find your way, to encourage you to get on the right plane—the one which will take you to *real success.*

Perhaps you've been blinded by the sight of palm trees. All your life you've lived in the mountains and just the sight of what seems like success is so good you've decided to stop at the first watering hole, rather than going on to discover God's best.

Maybe in your eagerness to find success, you've listened to someone who's offered you an easy way, and you have settled for some false religion.

Maybe you followed the crowd. After all, there are more people getting off in Tampa than in Melbourne, so why not go where everyone else seems to be going.

Or perhaps you're just afraid. You've heard all sorts of stories about people who followed God, who put their trust in Him. You don't want to become a fanatic, so you'll just spend your life in the Tampa airport, riding the escalators and looking out the windows at the waving palm trees.

Sound silly?

Sound familiar?

ELEVEN WHO HAVE FOUND SUCCESS

Maybe it would help if I introduced you to some folks who didn't allow worldly success to blind them from finding God's goal of success. This kind of success is a lasting success that no one can take away from them.

Jeff Gordon
PROFESSIONAL RACE-CAR
DRIVER

My wife, Brooke, and I each accepted Jesus Christ as our Saviour a few years ago. Now we cultivate our faith by reading Scripture (the Bible) and praying together. We look forward to our regular Saturday-night Bible study with some of the other race-car drivers and their wives.

My only regret is that I didn't become a Christian sooner. I didn't have God in my life when I needed Him ten years ago. I wish I had known more about the Bible and had read it. It could have made a big difference. And that's why I'm not shy about urging others to look into the claims of Christ and turn their lives over to Him.

How about you? Are you convinced yet of your own need for the Lord? If not, let me tell you about just one of the differences faith has made in my life.

Before I met Jesus, I was like most athletes—obsessed with winning. And when I didn't win, I felt discouraged and depressed. But now, when I have a bad day, I don't get upset, and I don't get frustrated. Sure, I'd like to have a better day; I want to win the race. But when I don't win, I don't get down. And I think that makes it easier for me to go to the next race.

Now, every race I go into, I'm content with whatever the outcome turns out to be. If I don't win that day, then God didn't want me to win that day. If I do win, I praise God for the victory. He's there with me all the time, win or lose!

The next time you see me competing in a race, you might remember this: When I'm out there and I'm racing hard, I'm not thinking about winning a trophy or making money or getting glory for myself. The only thing in my mind is doing my best and winning the race if I can—and always, in success or failure, glorifying God.

CHAPTER ONE

Reggie White
PROFESSIONAL FOOTBALL PLAYER

When I was a free agent considering offers from different pro football teams, I came home one day to this message on my answering machine: "Reggie, this is God. Go to Green Bay." I thought it was sort of suspicious that "God" sounded a lot like the Green Bay Packers' coach, Mike Holmgren.

Well, I did wind up going to Green Bay. But more to the point, I was pleased that my faith in God was well enough known in the football world that Coach could make a joke about it.

It all goes back to my childhood. My pastor at that time was the greatest man of God I've ever known. He had a way with kids and teaching. He helped me understand how to become a Christian by asking Jesus to forgive my sins and be my Saviour. I did that when I was thirteen, and afterwards I felt the peace of God in my life. I felt His forgiveness and His love for me.

Studying the Bible helped keep my life on track, even though there were bad influences like drugs and crime all around me. Reading about the trials of Christ made me more committed to serving Him.

There are some who say Christianity is for wimps, but as far as I'm concerned, Jesus was the toughest, bravest man who ever walked the face of this earth. Before He died on the cross, He could have snapped His fingers and everything would have been over. But He chose not to do that and instead died a painful death to pay for our sins. This is the kind of Lord I can follow.

I've had a lot of football success in my life, but I've discovered that what really matters is what's on the inside. My relationship with God is something real, something alive. He helps me each and every day, guiding me, helping me make the right decisions, comforting me when I fail.

You may not know much joy; you may have fears; you may feel empty; you may be searching for peace and hope. Listen, I've been there, and now I know the answer to the tough questions and problems you face. If you ask Christ to be the Lord of your life, you can have fellowship with God and the promise of an eternal life in Heaven.

You are missing out if you don't accept Jesus Christ as your Saviour. You are missing out on the greatest gift that God has ever given mankind.

Heather Whitestone McCallum
MISS AMERICA 1995

Even though I grew up in the church, I did not accept Jesus as my Saviour until I was sixteen. At that time, I asked Jesus to forgive my sins, and I began a personal relationship with Him. He was and still is my role model.

When I was eighteen months old, I lost my hearing. It took me six years to say my last name correctly. I started to take ballet at age five and dreamed of becoming a ballerina even though I couldn't hear music.

In 1994 at the Miss America Pageant, I danced ballet to a Christian song in front of forty million people on television and won the talent competition.

I was selected to be the first Miss America with a disability in its seventy-five-year history. The reason I believe I achieved my God-given dreams was because of my faith in Jesus. Matthew 17:20 says, "'You didn't have enough faith,' Jesus told them. 'I assure you, even if you had faith as small as a mustard seed, you could say to this mountain, "Move from here to there," and it would move. Nothing would be impossible.'"

Three years before I won the Miss America title, I competed for the Miss Deaf Alabama Pageant because I wanted to be part of the deaf world. I always felt left out in the hearing world. However, the judges told me that they could not consider me part of the deaf world because of my speaking ability. That pageant left me with an incredible feeling of emptiness. Over and over I prayed, "God, who am I? Hearing or deaf? Why do I have to be alone all my life?"

Then I read in the Bible about one of Jesus' disciples, Thomas—the disciple who needed to see Jesus' hands and feet in order to believe that He was the Saviour. Jesus said to him, "Blessed are those who haven't seen Me and believe."

Then I realized that no one could hear Jesus or see Him; everyone has to feel Him and hear His voice in his or her own heart. In God's eyes, I was just like everyone else. I knew that my deafness was a blessing from God.

I pray that those of you who doubt Jesus or are not happy with your life will open your heart to Jesus. There is no doubt that Jesus loves you, no matter what.

Christopher Parkening
CLASSICAL GUITARIST

I was raised in a "Christian" home, attended church, read the Bible occasionally, and was baptized at an early age. I thought I was a Christian, and yet my motives, purpose and lifestyle did not characterize what I now know to be Christian.

I began studying guitar at the age of eleven and by the time I was nineteen was fortunate to sign a contract with Capitol Records. The following year I signed with Columbia Artists Management, played over seventy-five concerts that year, and also founded the guitar department at the University of Southern California while attending school there.

Even before I began the guitar I had a great love of the outdoors, especially fly-fishing for trout. That's when I was the happiest. My goal was to own my own trout stream and retire at an early age. I worked very hard playing over ninety concerts a year and was finally able to buy my ranch and trout stream and retire at about the age of thirty.

I had everything I thought would make me happy, but I felt empty inside.

One day a neighbor invited me to a church where I heard a message entitled "Examine Yourselves Whether You Be in the Faith" from Matthew 7. Here Jesus says, "Many will say to Me when they die, 'Lord, Lord . . .' and I will say unto them, 'Depart from Me, I never knew you!'"

My life flashed before me, and I realized I would stand before Christ who would say to me, "Depart from Me, I never knew you! You never cared about obeying My commandments; you never cared about glorifying Me with your life or your music. All you cared about were your ranches and trout streams. Depart from Me!"

Suddenly I realized I wasn't a Christian after all! I knew the right facts about Christ, and even wanted a Saviour to save me from hell. What I did not want was a Lord of my life that I should follow, trust, and obey. Jesus must be both my Saviour and my Lord! So I gave my life to Christ, asked Him to forgive my sins and be my Lord and Saviour. By His grace alone He saved me. This was not something to be earned by being good, but it was God's gift to me as I repented and trusted in Jesus.

Soon after, I came across a verse in 1 Corinthians, which says, "Whatever you do, . . . do all for the glory of God" (1 Cor. 10:31). I started to play the guitar again, but this time for a different purpose: to honor and glorify my Lord and Saviour Jesus Christ.

Mary Joe Fernandez
PROFESSIONAL TENNIS PLAYER

One of the highest points and one of the lowest points in my life both occurred in the early 1990s. The high point was the 1992 Olympic Games in Barcelona, where I won a bronze medal in singles tennis and a gold medal in doubles. The low point was my abdominal surgery in 1993, which kept me bedridden for weeks and has led to a number of career-hindering health problems ever since then.

But something else was going on in my life around that time that was of more long-lasting importance and put everything else into perspective for me. That's when I made a commitment of my life to Jesus Christ.

Even though I grew up in a Christian home and had Christian values ingrained in me as a child, my "faith" wasn't really my own—it was more my parents'. So eventually I went through a time of soul-searching, looking for answers.

Two things helped me find those answers. I read the Gospel of John, as a friend recommended. I was also influenced by a book called *Power for Living*—yes, the earlier edition of the book you are now reading. As I read the stories of athletes and celebrities who had put their faith in Jesus Christ, it hit me that I too needed to turn my life over to the control of Christ. And that is just what I did!

Now I try to focus on having Jesus at the center of my life at all times. Everything I do is for His glory.

When I'm out on the court or whenever I'm struggling, I recite Psalm 27:1 to myself: *The Lord is my light and the one who saves me. I fear no one* (NCV). Growing up, I always thought I was in control, but through my newfound faith, I realized that isn't true. I can't do anything on my own, but I *can* do anything through Christ, who strengthens me.

As I've gone through illness, injuries, and other setbacks, it's helped me to know that while we don't see the whole plan, God does. And relying on Christ helps me get through the trials.

Perhaps you're going through struggles yourself. Perhaps you're where I was when I first read this book—searching for answers. If so, I urge you to give control of your life over to Jesus today. You'll never be sorry you did!

Bernhard Langer
PROFESSIONAL GOLFER

At the 1991 Ryder Cup—the Super Bowl of golf—it all came down to the last putt on the last hole in the last match on the last day. I faced a six-foot putt to win the cup—by far the most important stroke in my career. I missed.

Nightmares like that have been known to end careers because they shake a golfer's confidence so badly. But by having an eternal perspective, I was able to cope with it.

It was not always like that with me.

For a long time, my priorities were golf, golf, golf, and more golf. What little time was left over I gave to my wife and every now and then to the practice of my religion. If my golf game was not good, my whole life was miserable. When everything was going well in my game, I felt I didn't need God or anybody. But inside I always knew there was something missing.

Then in 1985 I was invited to attend the golfing tour's Bible study. My wife and I went. There we met a bunch of other professional golfers and their wives.

That evening was the first time I heard that I needed to be reborn to have eternal life. But I didn't understand it. So at the end of the study, I asked the leader of the study, Larry Moody, what he meant.

In practical terms Larry explained spiritual rebirth. He said that all people are separated from God because of their sin. He also said that lots of religious people think they can overcome this problem by doing good deeds for God (that was me!). But no one is so good that they can save themselves, and no one is so bad that God can't save them.

When I heard all this, it was natural to ask the Lord into my life. My wife, Vicki, felt the same way, and she also asked the Lord to save her. Since then I have seen tremendous changes in her life, in my life, in our relationship, and in the way we treat others.

My priorities have changed a lot since that day in 1985. Now they are God, my family, and my job. Every morning when I get up, I give my whole day over to the Lord. I'm never alone; He's always by my side.

It means a lot for me to represent my country in the Ryder Cup and other world championships. But it means much more to be a part of the team of Jesus Christ.

Andy Pettitte
PITCHER FOR THE NEW YORK YANKEES

If you're a major league pitcher, one thing is for certain. You're going to make mistakes. Believe me, it doesn't take much of a mistake for Ken Griffey to hit one out of the yard or for Mo Vaughn to smoke one off my forehead!

Sometimes after I've had a bad inning I'll think, *How can I be this bad? I must be the worst pitcher in this league.* After the game, when I have had a chance to really think about things the way I should, I realize where my significance comes from: It's not about my winning percentage, innings pitched, strikeouts, or World Series rings. Don't get me wrong—those things are good. But I know what makes me significant is Jesus Christ and my relationship to Him. I place my trust in Him (and not me). It still inspires awe and wonder in me to think about these words: "For God so loved the world that He gave His only Son, so that everyone who believes in Him will not perish but have eternal life" (John 3:16).

Pitching for the New York Yankees could be the ultimate roller coaster ride if you let it be. *This pitch is good. I'm happy. That pitch is bad. I stink. We win. I feel good. We lose. I'm depressed. The newspapers like me and think I'm good. I'm happy. Then I get knocked out of the game in the fifth.* Well, you get the idea. Jesus Christ was perfect, and I'm not. And I'm OK with that.

I'm grateful that God has helped me to avoid the big temptations that I have seen trip up some others. The big temptations are easy for me to avoid. There'll be no drugs, no infidelity, and there will be lots of accountability.

I have always tried to discipline myself to avoid the more subtle temptations, like falling into a "star" mentality or lowering my standards of how I should treat people around me. I know God hates the sin of pride and arrogance. I have also seen how easy it can be for professional athletes to think they are entitled to superstar treatment. I know I don't want to go there—it could be a deep hole that's hard to climb out of.

I know that God is good and that He has a plan. Here's my game plan: to give my life to Jesus Christ (I did that several years ago), to be a faithful and loving child of God, and to do my best as a professional athlete and husband and father. I will always try to stay close to Him. And if we happen to win the World Series again, well, that would be just fine, too.

Jackie Joyner-Kersee
TRACK STAR

When I was fourteen, watching the 1976 Olympics on television, I never dreamed God would ask me to literally "run the race that is before us" (Hebrews 12:1, NCV). I didn't know I was going to be a world record holder and a gold medalist. But I had my family, friends, and mentors who believed in me and showed me that, through hard work, good choices, a determination to never give up, and especially a firm faith in God, I could be successful. And that's made all the difference!

East St. Louis was a typical inner-city area when I grew up; and my parents saw to it that my siblings and I developed positive and healthy personality traits. They based their teachings on having a tremendous faith in the Lord and love. It was clear that Jesus was the guiding force in our family life. On Sunday we went to church and Sunday school, no questions asked. And we looked forward to it. With the influence of my family and my church, I accepted Christ as a young child. The people at that church became mentors for me.

While athletics has consumed a big part of my life, I try not to let my athletic accomplishments change who I am inside. I've gained a lot of material things from athletics, but I know that's not what matters long-term. It's my soul, my character, the God I stand for that mean more to me than anything in the world. I hope the people I interact with see that in me.

Although I do share my faith with audiences, I realize that actions speak louder than words. If I'm being true to who I am as a child of God, people will know I'm a Christian from the way I act. I don't change like a chameleon for different environments, depending on whom I'm talking to. My faith doesn't waver.

When my life gets tough, the Bible encourages me to continue believing in God's goodness. I keep exercising my faith, even when the road ahead isn't clear. I'm learning to accept the good with the bad—whatever God allows—to help me grow.

No matter how many medals I win, I'm still Jackie. I'll never forget where I came from or what it took to get me where I am now. God is the one who gave me my success—and He can take it away if I don't handle it well. Knowing where my true success and self-worth come from puts my life in the right perspective.

God, my husband, and I are a team. I thank God first for my success, because He's been with me all the way. One of my favorite verses is Philippians 4:13: "I can do all things through Christ because he gives me strength" (NCV).

Kenneth H. Cooper, M.D.
"THE FATHER OF AEROBICS"

In 1968, I wrote the book *Aerobics,* then two years later founded the Cooper Aerobics Center in Dallas, Texas. Back then hardly anybody knew what *aerobics* meant; now it's a household word. It's been the mission of my life to help people improve their physical health through conditioning aerobics programs.

The basic purpose of doing aerobic exercise is to prevent illness and debilitation by maintaining the health and strength of the body. Many of us discover that we cannot live our life to the full unless we keep our body in good condition. Physical health is important to you, me, and everybody.

But something else I like to tell people is that the health of the body is not everything. The health of the soul matters much more.

When I was still a child, I realized that my inner life was not all it could have been. Something was missing, and I knew that the absence of that "something"—whatever it was—was preventing me from living life as I wanted to live it.

I was raised in a Christian home, so as I searched for the missing piece in my life, I naturally began to read the Bible. There I discovered that I could enjoy true happiness and peace of mind only if I had a personal relationship with Jesus Christ. That's when I invited the Lord to come into my heart and take control of my life.

Ever since then my life with God has been an adventure as He has directed me and used me in ways I never could have anticipated. Let me give you just one example of that.

As a young man, I desired to be a medical missionary to China. But as the years passed, somehow I never pursued that dream. Then in 1990 I had the opportunity to travel throughout China and address large audiences on the subject of aerobic fitness. Everywhere I spoke in this officially atheistic country, I mentioned Jesus Christ and my faith in Him, just as I normally do whenever I give speeches. Suddenly, I realized that in this way I was having a much broader witness to Christ in China than I ever would have had if I were a missionary doctor in some rural Chinese village. Isn't God wonderful?

Helping others improve their health is without question very important to me. But an even greater privilege is telling people how Jesus Christ has made my life complete. You, too, can be made complete simply by inviting the Lord into your life.

What a great joy it is to have good spiritual as well as physical health!

Don Nickles
UNITED STATES SENATOR

Shortly after I was first elected to the United States Senate, I was in Williamsburg, Virginia, with my family to make a speech. That evening my wife, Linda, and I were getting ready for a banquet while our four children were with the babysitter in the adjacent room.

Suddenly the babysitter cried out, "Senator Nickles, come here quick! Your daughter is in trouble!"

I dashed into the other room to find Kim, my five-year-old daughter barely conscious and staring at me with a scary look in her eyes. Something was lodged in her throat. Almost without thinking, I told Linda to call an ambulance, and I started to perform the Heimlich maneuver, squeezing Kim around the diaphragm to dislodge whatever was blocking her airway.

I knew there was really no chance that the ambulance would get there in time. It was apparent that Kim had not been breathing for some time and she might not survive.

"Dear God," I prayed desperately, "I'll do anything if you will give me back my daughter. Please don't let her die!" As

24

I squeezed harder and harder, I was afraid I might break her ribs.

Crying and praying, I gave one last thrust to her diaphragm. Suddenly, a circular piece of ice popped out of her mouth. She began to take in air in gasps. Her eyes were full of tears, and I drew her up in my arms and held her close to me.

She began to feel better, but I was trembling and quite shaken. Then I recalled how I had promised God that I would do anything if He would give me back my daughter. He had done that. He answered my prayer.

As I was still holding my daughter, an incredible thought occurred to me. I would give anything for my daughter—certainly my own life. But would I be willing to give her life for someone else? No way! But as I had heard from my mother and other Christians, that is exactly what God did for us. He loved us so much that He gave His only Son to die for us. What an unbelievable gift! It's beyond comprehension. But at that moment, it became very real to me.

I never realized how much God loves you and me—more than we can imagine—even more than we love our own children! That night I recommitted my life to God. I know by accepting God's gift of His Son Jesus that my sins have been paid for and forgiven and that I will be with God eternally. If you have never made the same commitment to God, now is the time. It's a free gift. All you have to do is say yes.

Arthur S. DeMoss

1925–1979
DECEASED FOUNDER AND C.E.O.
NATIONAL LIBERTY CORPORATION[1]

As a young person I always wanted to get all the thrills and excitement I could out of life. And I don't think there was anything wrong with that, but, not being a Christian at the time, I didn't know how to go about it right.

The thing that excited me most in my early teens was gambling. It started with cards we had around the house, and soon I was betting on racehorses, roulette, baseball, football—anything for action. I loved it. I thought I could quit breathing before I could quit gambling.

Then, in pursuit of other thrills, I began traveling. By the time I was sixteen, I had been in more than forty states as well as Canada and Mexico. I remember writing to my parents from Las Vegas (the gamblers' Mecca at that time), telling them I'd found heaven and not to expect me home soon. It broke my parents' hearts.

I had the good fortune of coming from an excellent home. As a child, I attended church and Sunday school. I also went to one of the country's finest prep schools. But somehow my upbringing and education didn't make life more satisfying or meaningful.

Much to the dismay of my parents and teachers, in my late teens I opened a couple of "horse rooms" in my hometown of Albany, New York. I soon found myself handling bets totaling upwards of $10,000[2] a day.

By the time I was twenty-four, I had four offices, and in that year I bought three Cadillac convertibles. But along with these things there was a void inside me. I didn't realize that my problem was a spiritual one because I had always believed in God. But I wasn't a Christian and had never heard of being born-again.

One night, just for a change from the routine of the racetracks and nightclubs and country clubs, I went to a meeting where I heard a lawyer talk about Jesus Christ in a way that really gripped me. This was what I had always been searching for—I had just been looking in the wrong places. So I asked Christ to forgive my sins and to come into my heart and life. That was the greatest night in all my life—Friday, October 13, 1950.

Since then, every day has been thrilling and exciting. I've found that the greatest excitement in this life comes from sharing my faith with others and seeing them find the Saviour. Today, I'd much rather tell others about God's Eternal Life Insurance than to sell millions of dollars' worth of earthly life insurance which my company offers!

[1] Mr. DeMoss's company, the National Liberty Corporation, was listed on the New York Stock Exchange and was acquired by Capital Holding Corporation after his death.

[2] Today's equivalent, $161,000 a day.

There you have it . . . the words of eleven who made it to real success. These are people who didn't get off the plane at the wrong stop.

Did you notice what they had in common? All realized they were failures without God—even though all were quite successful by this world's standards. They all had a personal relationship with Jesus Christ and a profound respect for the Bible as the Word of God.

You ask, "But how does this apply to me?"

I've shared their lives with you for one reason—to let you know that you, too, can find power for living. That's what this book is all about. So I encourage you to read on. We've just begun to share with you how you can reach the right destination . . . how you can change your life and reach the goal of real success—a goal which God wants you to reach, also.

So if you've gotten off the plane at the wrong stop—or maybe taken the wrong flight altogether—then this book is for you. The desires of your heart can be met. You can find power for living.

Then God said, "Let us make people in our image, to be like ourselves. They will be masters over all life—the fish in the sea, the birds in the sky and all the livestock, wild animals, and small animals."

Genesis 1:26

YOU ARE SPECIAL TO GOD

There is a legend among the Cheyenne Indians of an isolated village on the edge of a forest. For years the adults in the village had practiced a little routine. One by one they would sneak out of the village and follow a small path through the forest to a silver stream. There was a log over the stream which had been worn smooth by many moccasined feet. Looking around to make sure no one was looking, the Indian would walk out on the log. Looking down into the silver stream, he would see his reflection. Then, in a quiet voice, he would begin to talk. He would tell the stream all the deep things of his heart. Doing this made him feel good. When he was finished, he would return to the village.

Even though all the adult Indians did this on a regular basis, they never told anyone. However, everyone seemed to know everyone else was doing the same thing.

One day two Indian children found the path into the woods. Curious, they followed it and soon found the silver stream. Seeing the log over the stream, they walked out on it and looked down. There, in the water, they saw the reflection of their faces. Before long they were talking to the stream, telling it all the deep things of their hearts. It made them feel good. Very good.

Running down the path, they entered the village and called the adults together. But when they told the adults what they had discovered and what they had done, the adults were offended—and threatened. They took up stones and chased the children out of the village.

The meaning of the legend, according to the Cheyenne, is that everyone needs someone to talk to, someone to relate to, someone to whom you can tell all the deep things of your heart. But since that is also considered a sign of weakness, you dare not let anyone else know.

The Indians are half right. We are created with a deep need to relate. Someone once said that inside every man is a little boy still trying to please his father. I guess the same thing applies to the little girl who resides inside every woman. Inside all of us is a child who desperately needs to lean on God.

But our society has done a strange thing. It has conditioned us to look upon dependence on God as a sign of weakness. We see "success" as the ability to go it alone, to make it without anyone's help—especially God's help. Therefore, when we hear someone say, "I surrendered to God," or "I asked Jesus to take control of my life," we immediately think of the person as a weakling, a washout, a failure who couldn't make it on his or her own and had to call on God for help.

This is basically a Western concept, by the way. Most people in Third World nations, and nearly all those who live in the East, see dependence on the "spirit world" as a natural part of living. It's only Europeans and Americans, with our strong sense of independence, who are reluctant to call upon

God for help. Yet, like the Indians, when we get alone and are honest—standing on the log, looking down into the silver stream, there is a strong urge to speak the deep things of our heart. And when we do, we feel good inside; for inside every human being there is a small voice which whispers, telling us despite what the world says, God loves us and we are special to Him.

Our problem is pride. We don't want to admit that we're incapable of handling life's problems alone.

Charlie Brown is constantly struggling with this. One day Charlie Brown was talking to his friend, Linus, about the pervasive sense of inadequacy he feels all the time. "You see, Linus," Charlie Brown moaned, "it goes all the way back to the beginning. The moment I was born and set foot on the stage of life they took one look at me and said, 'Not right for the part.'"

How many of us, like Charlie Brown, have looked in the mirror and concluded we were "not right for the part"?

It was Charlie Brown who complained to Linus about his publisher. "The publisher sent me a rejection slip," lamented Charlie Brown.

"So what?" said Linus. "Lots of writers get rejection slips."

"But I didn't even submit a manuscript," cried Charlie Brown.

It's that kind of feeling which can quickly turn into an attitude—the attitude of rejection and inadequacy. But this is a perversion of the truth. It is a lie, constantly whispered to us by the devil, to convince us we are really not created in the image of God, that we are not precious to God, that even though Jesus Christ may have died on a cross, He didn't do it for me. If the lie is not corrected, if the attitude is not checked, it could easily lead to depression or worse.

Cartoonists are constantly playing on this aspect of life. In Al Capp's comic strip, "Li'l Abner," there was a strange little character who had a dark cloud which hung over his head and accompanied him everywhere. As a result, wherever this pathetic little fellow went, there were disasters which followed. Trucks ran off bridges. Pianos fell out of skyscrapers. People dropped into open manholes. We used to laugh at this poor little Joe, but only because we saw ourselves in him.

Many in today's world feel they live under such a curse. It is like a dark shadow which is always with them. Eventually, they feel, it will catch up with them and consume them.

The fact is, that's not too far from wrong. The Bible tells us that all people are "sinners," that is, they are trying to live apart from God and His laws. This leads to a deep separation from God. As a result, since all good things come from God, it is difficult for the natural person to experience anything of lasting good.

King David, who had just had a good look at himself when the prophet Nathan came along and pointed out some evil things in his life, confessed an eternal truth when he said, ***"For I was born a sinner—yes, from the moment my mother conceived me"*** (Psalms 51:5).

That's a powerful confession, and one that is profoundly true. In other words, David took a good look at himself and said, "Not right for the part."

If we were to diagram this, we'd do it by making a chart with lines extending out in all directions saying, "I'm not OK," "You're not OK," "We're not OK," "They're not OK," "It's not OK."

Now if you had not been a sinner from birth, then you could change that to say, "I'm OK, you're OK, we're all OK, and everything's dandy."

But that's not the way it is according to the Bible. The fact is that *"all have sinned; all fall short of God's glorious standard"* (Romans 3:23).

It is this "sin" which separates us from God and keeps us from being the success God intends for us to be. Therefore, before we do anything else, we need to take care of the *sin problem* in our lives.

Maybe it will be easier to understand if I describe it in terms of a man with his golf club. In the hands of a skilled golfer, a golf club can be used to knock a ball from the tee down the fairway, onto the green, and into the cup. But that's not possible if the golf club has been misused. Say it's been used to pry open the garage door, or maybe your son left it in the gutter and it was run over by the garbage truck. Now the head is cracked open and the shaft is bent so it looks like a Z. No matter how much the golfer wants to use it in the tournament, he'll never be able to play golf using that club.

That's what sin does to our lives. It makes us unusable. It causes us to give in to defeat and say, "So what. Forget about it. Tomorrow you die anyway. So eat, drink, and sleep with Mary."

But even though King David got honest with himself and recognized he was a sinner, he didn't stop there. He called out to God for cleansing and asked God to create in him a pure heart. In short, he asked God to *"wash me clean from my guilt. Purify me from my sin"* (Psalms 51:2).

You see, we all have a choice. To live God's way—or to live our way.

Several years ago a man wrote a book in which he said the most important thing on earth is "looking out for Number One." On the dedication page of the book he wrote: "Dedicated to the hope that somewhere in our universe there exists a civilization where the inhabitants possess sole dominion over their own lives."

There is such a place. It's called hell. It is the place where men have totally divorced themselves from God's claim on their lives.

But the truly successful person has learned that in order to have power for living—supernatural power for living—he must be properly related to God.

Psychologists tell us there are, built into each of us, five basic needs. These are needs for:

1. Security
2. Recognition
3. Love
4. Adventure
5. Creativity

These are sometimes called "drives." These drives, either individually or through a combination, control our lives. They are neither good nor evil. They are simply part of human nature. But it is these drives which cause us to walk out on a log in the forest and speak to the stream, telling it the deep things of our heart. It is these drives which, in the end, either push us into the arms of a loving Heavenly Father or, because we seek their fulfillment in some selfish or perverted way, drive us into hell.

If you don't find your answers to these drives in God, your human nature will force you to find them elsewhere—apart from God. It is when these drives are not met in God that you begin to feel inadequate—defeated. You feel like Charlie Brown: "Not right for the part."

It will always be this way until you enter the Kingdom of God. But once you've entered that Kingdom through a personal relationship with God, you are right for the part. From that time on you can say with confidence: "I am numbered among those who have been called by God. I have been chosen. I have a place in history."

Surely this is part of what being "born again" must mean. It means we're special to God.

Several years ago Fred Craddock was lecturing at Yale University. He told of going back one summer to Gatlinburg, Tennessee, to take a short vacation with his wife. One night they found a quiet little restaurant where they looked forward to a private meal—just the two of them.

While they were waiting for their meal, they noticed a distinguished looking, white-haired man moving from table to table, visiting guests. Craddock whispered to his wife, "I hope he doesn't come over here." He didn't want the man to intrude on their privacy.

But the man did come by his table.

"Where you folks from?" he asked amicably.

"Oklahoma."

"Splendid state, I hear, although I've never been there. What do you do for a living?"

"I teach homiletics at the graduate seminary of Phillips University."

"Oh, so you teach preachers, do you. Well, I've got a

story I want to tell you." And with that he pulled up a chair and sat down at the table with Craddock and his wife.

Dr. Craddock said he groaned inwardly. *Oh no, here comes another preacher story. It seems everyone has one.*

The man stuck out his hand. "I'm Ben Hooper. I was born not far from here across the mountains. My mother wasn't married when I was born so I had a hard time. When I started to school, my classmates had a name for me, and it wasn't a very nice name. I used to go off by myself at recess and during lunchtime because the taunts of my playmates cut so deeply.

"What was worse was going downtown on Saturday afternoon and feeling every eye burning a hole through me. They were all wondering just who my real father was.

"When I was about 12 years old, a new preacher came to our church. I would always go in late and slip out early. But one day the preacher said the benediction so fast I got caught and had to walk out with the crowd. I could feel every eye in church on me. Just about the time I got to the door, I felt a big hand on my shoulder. I looked up and the preacher was looking right at me.

" 'Who are you, son? Whose boy are you?'

"I felt the old weight come on me. It was like a big, black cloud. Even the preacher was putting me down.

"But as he looked down at me, studying my face, he began to smile a big smile of recognition. 'Wait a minute,' he said, 'I know who you are. I see the family resemblance. You are a son of God.'

"With that he slapped me across the rump and said, 'Boy, you've got a great inheritance. Go and claim it.' "

The old man looked across the table at Fred Craddock

and said, "That was the most important single sentence ever said to me." With that he smiled, shook the hands of Craddock and his wife, and moved on to another table to greet old friends.

Suddenly, Fred Craddock remembered that the people of Tennessee had elected an illegitimate to be their governor. His name was Ben Hooper.

That's what it means to be chosen by God. Although we have been born in iniquity, and although we have chosen to go our own way, through the blood of Jesus Christ we are saved—not only from our past, but from the fear of failure in our present and from powerless living in our future as well.

We have a great inheritance. The power for living that comes to us from God enables us to go and claim it.

For if you confess with your mouth that Jesus is Lord and believe in your heart that God raised Him from the dead, you will be saved. For it is by believing in your heart that you are made right with God, and it is by confessing with your mouth that you are saved.

Romans 10:9-10

HOW TO GET RIGHT WITH GOD

In the last chapter I pointed out that you are special to God. In fact, you are so special, God sent His Son, Jesus Christ, so you can have power for living. This cost Jesus His life, but by His death—and His resurrection from the dead—you can not only be forgiven and have eternal life, but you can have the power to overcome fear and live abundantly here on earth.

As a child I had two great fears. One was the fear of being left alone. The other was the fear of the unknown.

I was always afraid I would have to go live with my uncle and aunt in Indiana. These fears haunted me day and night.

I remember the night I was left home with my mother while my father was out of town. My mother was sick, and when I tried to help her get out of bed to go to the bathroom, she fainted on the floor. She was too heavy for me to move. I had the presence of mind to call our family doctor, who was an old friend and lived not too far from our rural house. He came over, got my mother back into her bed, and told me not to be afraid.

But I was afraid. I stayed awake all night, my nose pressed against the screen in the window, wishing my father would pull up in the driveway so I wouldn't have to be alone.

I was also terrified by the fear of the unknown. Occasionally our family would drive north from our home in Florida to visit my mother's relatives in Kentucky, or to pay a visit to my father's sister in Indiana. I dreaded those trips because we always spent the night in tourist homes on the road. Those were the days before motels were popular. Instead, travelers stayed in what were called tourist homes or rooming houses in the small towns on the way. These were usually big, old houses which an old couple, or perhaps a widow, would open up to take in overnight lodgers.

I dreaded staying in these strange homes. Invariably I would have to stay in a room at the end of the hall on the third floor. If I was fortunate I got to sleep in the same bed with my younger brother. The beds were usually creaky, old, iron-poster beds with exposed metal springs. The walls would be covered with the pictures of people who no doubt had lived and died in that same room. All through the night I would waken and see them staring down at me from their dusty picture frames.

Equally frightening was rain at night. It was always a terrifying situation to drive into a strange city at night with the rain peppering against the windshield. I would huddle close to my daddy and wish I were back in the familiar surroundings of my home in Florida.

That all came back to me last winter when I went on

a hunting trip with some of my friends deep in the Florida Everglades. One of the men in the group owned a small cabin perched in a clump of live oaks and cabbage palms called a "hammock." This was surrounded on all sides by low, marshy ground. As far as the eye could see there was swamp, dotted with these "hammocks"—all of which looked alike.

The first afternoon we were there, one of the men took us out into the swamp in a Jeep with oversized tires. He let each man off at a separate deer stand, about a mile apart and approximately two miles from the cabin. He promised to come back before dark to pick us up.

Shortly before dark it began to rain—a soft, misting rain. I pulled my rifle under my poncho and snuggled against the trunk of the huge oak tree where I was perched on a limb, high off the ground. It began to get dark, and I could hear the raindrops dripping loudly on the palm fronds below me. I began to think, *What am I doing up here in this tree in the middle of the Everglades when I could be home in my nice warm bed instead? Besides, I don't even like to kill things. The only reason I'm here is to be with my son, Tim, who is getting ready to leave for college. And I'm not even with him because he's on a deer stand on the other side of the swamp.*

I slipped down out of the tree and started back to the cabin. The rain was falling harder now, and darkness had totally enveloped the swamp. I made my way through the thick hammock where I had been sitting and across an open glade. I was sloshing through ankle-deep water in tall grass looking for the barbed-wire fence which marked the edge of the section where we were hunting.

But now it was completely dark. I found the fence where my friend was supposed to pick me up, but there was no sign of a truck. Perhaps he had already come by and, thinking I had walked back to the cabin, gone on. I had no choice but to try to find my way back to the cabin in the dark.

Finding some higher ground along the fence line, I slogged on through the misting rain, following the fence to a gate. I knew at that point I had to turn left across an open glade and walk about a mile. But there were no landmarks. No stars. Only the dark, shadowy silhouettes of the various hammocks against the darkening horizon. I searched the ground, found the impressions of the truck tires, and set off across the glade in a hopeless quest of following the tire tracks in the dark. I knew the cabin was located in one of those dark clumps of trees but had no idea which one. I was literally feeling my way when it occurred to me I was lost. Unless someone came out looking for me, I just might have to spend the night in the swamp.

I waited for the old feelings of fear to set in, the gnawing in the pit of my stomach, the sting of tears in my eyes—all the old sensations I used to have as a child when I was left alone or was in a strange place. But there was nothing. No fear. No anxiety. Just a simple resignation that if I had to spend the night in the swamp I'd better try and find a dry spot.

I stumbled upon a small cattle feeder, a little shed-like structure which protected a block of salt for the range cows that wandered free in this section of the swamp. But as I knelt down to see if it was dry under the little roof, I spotted, far in the distance, a light shining through the trees in one of the hammocks. It was our cabin. In a short while I was safe in the warm, dry house, preparing for a dinner of smoked turkey with my friends—all of whom (including my son) thought it was a great joke that I had been lost in the dark.

That night, lying on my cot, listening in the darkness to the rain drizzling on the tin roof of the cabin, I reflected on my feelings. What had happened to the old fear? Where was the old gut-wrenching terror of the past? It wasn't until the next morning that I fully realized what had happened to me.

I was back on the deer stand at dawn. Only this time I didn't climb up in my tree. I leaned my unloaded rifle on a log and stood at the edge of the woods, watching the sun come up, listening as the world came alive at dawn. Moments before it had been totally silent. Not a sound, not a leaf moving. Then, as the eastern sky began to turn first light blue, then a soft rose color, a bird chirped. Then a squirrel moved. I heard the rustle of a raccoon family coming through the tall grass. An armadillo scurried in front of me, his long nose probing the ground for grubs and beetles. Butterflies and mosquito hawks sailed gracefully overhead. Next came the sound of many birds chirping; squirrels barked in the trees and scampered along the low branches of the big oaks. And in the distance I heard the gobbling of a flock of wild turkeys.

Then, on the far side of the small glade where I was standing, I spotted him—a magnificent buck. He was standing head erect, his rack of horns crowning his regal head. He sniffed the air, looked directly at me and slowly

45

Don't be afraid, for I am with you.
Do not be dismayed, for I am your God.
I will strengthen you. I will help you.
I will uphold you with My victorious right hand.

Isaiah 41:10

turned and entered the woods. He and I were part of the same creation—citizens of this marvelous garden of nature.

I stood for long moments, scarcely breathing, my heart beating in tune with all the sounds around me. The rain the night before had sweetened the air and freshened the earth. The golden sun rose in the east behind the clumps of cabbage palms, and suddenly the entire earth was alive with color and sound. I heard myself singing an old hymn:

> When morning gilds the skies
> My heart awakening cries,
> May Jesus Christ be praised.
>
> The night becomes as day,
> When from the heart we say,
> May Jesus Christ be praised.
>
> The powers of darkness fear
> When this sweet chant they hear:
> May Jesus Christ be praised.

That's it. The powers of darkness no longer had dominion over me. Why? Because a number of years before, I had given my life to Jesus Christ. That which used to terrify me no longer controlled me. Now, through Jesus, I had power for living. I had appropriated what the apostle Paul had told his young friend, Timothy: ***"For God has not given us a spirit of fear and timidity, but of power, love, and self-discipline"*** (2 Timothy 1:7).

How does one give his life to Jesus Christ? How can you come into this intimate fellowship with the Lord God of the universe who takes away our fear and replaces it with power?

Just as there are physical laws that govern the physical universe—causing the rain to fall and the sun to rise—so there are spiritual laws which govern your relationship with God. Submitting to these laws will allow Jesus Christ to become the Lord of your life. When that happens, He replaces your old power with His supernatural power for living.

LAW ONE:

God loves you and offers a wonderful plan for your life.

GOD'S LOVE

"For God so loved the world that He gave His only Son, so that everyone who believes in Him will not perish but have eternal life" (John 3:16).

GOD'S PLAN

(Jesus speaking) *"My purpose is to give life in all its fullness"* (John 10:10).

But as we've already seen, simply knowing that God loves you and has a wonderful plan for your life isn't enough. There are things which block us from God's love. And that brings us to the next law.

LAW TWO:

Man is sinful and separated from God.

Because of this he cannot know and experience God's love and God's plan for his life.

MAN IS SINFUL

"For all have sinned; all fall short of God's glorious standard" (Romans 3:23).

You see, man was created to have fellowship with God. Just as I was able to stand in the Everglades and feel God's presence all around me without fear, so God wants you to have fellowship with Him. It is the same kind of fellowship Adam and Eve had with God in the Garden of Eden before sin entered the world. There, these two friends of God walked with Him in the cool of the evening, talking with their Creator as a son and daughter talk to their daddy.

But then Adam and Eve decided to go their own way rather than God's way. They broke fellowship with God, and ever since then man has chosen to go his own independent way. Sometimes this self-will is exercised in active rebellion against God. Sometimes it is expressed in passive indifference toward God. In whatever form it appears, this self-will is what the Bible calls *sin.*

MAN IS SEPARATED

"For the wages of sin is death, but the free gift of God is eternal life through Christ Jesus our Lord" (Romans 6:23).

This diagram illustrates that God is holy and man is sinful. A great gulf separates the two. The arrows illustrate that man continually tries to reach God and the abundant life through his own efforts, such as living a good life, philosophy or even religion. The third law explains the only way we can bridge this gulf.

LAW THREE:

Jesus Christ is God's only provision for man's sin.

Through Him you can know and experience God's love and God's plan for your life.

HE DIED IN OUR PLACE

"But God showed His great love for us by sending Christ to die for us while we were still sinners" (Romans 5:8).

HE ROSE FROM THE DEAD

"Christ died for our sins. . . . He was buried, and He was raised from the dead on the third day, as the Scriptures said. He was seen by Peter and then by the twelve apostles. After that, He was seen by more than five hundred" (1 Corinthians 15:3-6).

HE IS THE ONLY WAY TO GOD

"Jesus told him, 'I am the way, the truth, and the life. No one can come to the Father except through me' " (John 14:6).

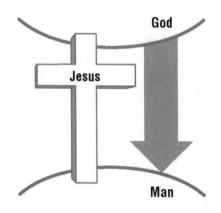

This diagram illustrates that God has bridged the gulf which separates us from Him by sending His Son, Jesus Christ, to die on the cross in our place—to pay the penalty for our sins. But it is not enough to know these three laws. We also need to know the fourth one.

LAW FOUR:

We must individually receive Jesus Christ as Saviour and Lord.

Then we can know and experience God's love and plan for our lives.

WE MUST RECEIVE CHRIST
"But to all who believed Him and accepted Him, He gave the right to become children of God" (John 1:12).

WE MUST RECEIVE CHRIST THROUGH FAITH
"God saved you by His special favor when you believed. And you can't take credit for this; it is a gift from God. Salvation is not a reward for the good things we have done, so none of us can boast about it" (Ephesians 2:8-9).

WHEN WE RECEIVE CHRIST, WE EXPERIENCE NEW BIRTH
"Jesus replied, 'I assure you, unless you are born again, you can never see the Kingdom of God'" (John 3:3).

WE RECEIVE CHRIST BY PERSONAL INVITATION
"Look! Here I stand at the door and knock. If you hear me calling and open the door, I will come in, and we will share a meal as friends" (Revelation 3:20).

Receiving Christ means we have to turn to Him. In order to do this, we have to turn away from our sin. We cannot do this in our own power. But we must be willing to relinquish our sin and to surrender to Him all the rights to our life. Then, in an act of faith, we invite Jesus Christ to take over the control of our life. While that may seem difficult, it is in reality a very simple thing. All you do is, by an act of your will, say, "I want You, Jesus, to take over my life."

If you mean it with all your heart—He will.

Let me illustrate it by these two circles which represent two kinds of lives: the self-directed life and the Christ-directed life.

SELF-DIRECTED LIFE
S—Self is on the throne
†—Christ is outside
•—Interests are directed by self, often resulting in discord and frustration

CHRIST-DIRECTED LIFE
†—Christ is in the life and on the throne
S—Self is yielding to Christ
•—Interests are directed by Christ, resulting in harmony with God's plan

Which circle best represents your life?

Which circle would you like to have represent your life?

HOW YOU CAN RECEIVE JESUS CHRIST

When you stop and realize you were created by God for one purpose—so you could have fellowship with Him—then it stands to reason that God's greatest purpose for you is to have that fellowship restored. How is this done? It happens when you accept God's Son, Jesus Christ, as your Lord—the One who will—from this time on—direct your life.

"Well," you ask, "does that mean I have to join a church? What about the bad habits in my life? Don't I have to give them up before I'm worthy to have fellowship with God?

"I've done too many bad things. I don't believe God will take me the way I am. Don't I have to do something first before He'll receive me?"

Let's put these questions aside for a while, because right now they don't make any difference. All of them are based on the presupposition you have to *do* something before God will receive you. But remember the Scripture verse we looked at a moment ago from Ephesians? It pointed out that our relationship with God is not "a reward for the good things we have done," but it is a "gift from God." None of us could ever earn or deserve God's love and forgiveness. But He makes it freely available to anyone who will stop trusting in his own good works and efforts and will place all his faith in Jesus Christ to save him.

The wonderful thing is that you don't have to wait for God to receive you. He is waiting for you to receive Him.

Here's how you do it. You simply get alone somewhere and tell God that you believe in Him, that you cannot go on living without Him, that you are now accepting Jesus Christ as your Lord, and that from this time on you are going to allow Jesus to sit on the throne of your life.

Here's a simple prayer you can pray. In fact, if after reading this prayer it voices how you feel, you can read it over again and make it *your* prayer. When you do that, God will hear you—and Jesus will come into your life as Lord.

> Dear God, I've been living my life my own way. Now I want to live it Your way. I need You and I am now willing for You to take control of my life. I receive Your Son Jesus Christ, as my personal Saviour and Lord. I believe He died for my sins and has risen from the dead. I surrender to Him as Lord. Come, Lord Jesus, and occupy the throne of my life. Make me the kind of person You want me to be.

That's all there is to it. Oh, there's much more to come, and that's what the rest of this book is all about. But right here is where it all begins. And now that you've accepted Christ, and have allowed Him to move onto the throne of your life, you should *expect* some tremendous changes to take place. We'll be talking about those changes, too, and what you can expect.

You see, as a new citizen of the Kingdom of God, you have certain rights and privileges you've never had before. These are exciting things, for Christianity is not just a matter of *surrendering,* it is also a matter of receiving the marvelous gifts Jesus brings with Him when He takes control of your life. In fact, the moment that you received Christ as an act of faith, many things happened, including the following:

FIRST, Christ came into your life. Have you seen one of those little cars in the toy store? It looks real enough, but if you examine the box it came in, you'll see a little notice: "Batteries not included." Without batteries—no matter how authentic it looks—it won't run. You are made in the image of God but because of sin your batteries never did work. When Christ came into your life, He brought His power with Him.

Look at the words of Jesus. *"Look! Here I stand at the door and knock. If you hear Me calling and open the door, I will come in, and we will share a meal as friends"* (Revelation 3:20). Paul says it this way: *"Christ lives in you, and this is your assurance that you will share in His glory"* (Colossians 1:27). That's exciting. And very powerful.

SECOND, your sins were forgiven. When my oldest daughter was about two years old she climbed up on my dresser and found a ring which had been given me by my father. It was not a valuable ring, but it had a lot of sentimental meaning to me. Robin played with it for a while, then flushed it down the toilet. The next day, when I asked if anyone had seen my ring, she admitted her sin. Even though I punished her, I was unable to forgive her. The ring was that meaningful to me.

The next afternoon I came in from work and settled in my chair with the newspaper. When I looked up, there stood my four-year-old son. Beside him, with tears on her cheeks, was little Robin. Bruce did the talking. "Robin's sorry she lost your ring, Daddy. But we made you a new one this afternoon."

He held out his hand. In it was a ring—braided out of pine needles.

I swept them both into my arms and held them close to my chest. Not once since that time have I missed my old ring, nor have I ever again blamed my daughter for what she did. Because of the action of her brother, she was forgiven. Totally.

That is what Jesus did for us. He went to the Father and paid the price for our sin. Because of Him, Paul says in Colossians 1:14, *"God has purchased our freedom with His blood and has forgiven all our sins."*

THIRD, you became a child of God. In fact, the Bible says, you now have the same rights as the Son of God, Jesus Christ. These are inherited rights because you are now an heir of God and a joint heir with Jesus Christ. *"But to all who believed Him and accepted Him, He gave the right to become children of God,"* one of Jesus' biographers tells us in John 1:12.

Something like this happened to my younger sister. After my parents had four sons, they decided to adopt a little girl. She was only a few days old when my mother brought her home from the hospital. Although a woman other than his wife had given birth to her, my father fully accepted Audrey as his own child. She grew up as a Buckingham and has shared equally in everything belonging to the family.

Recently I was meeting with a group of men at a retreat lodge near where Audrey lives in Missouri. One afternoon she drove out to the retreat center to visit me. Although none of the men in the group had ever met her before—in fact, none of them even knew I had a sister—when she showed up at the retreat center looking for me several men recognized her as my sister.

Across the years we've even begun to look alike. She is my father's daughter and she's fully accepted into the family.

FOURTH, you received eternal life. That may not mean much to you right now, but in the long run it is the most important thing that can ever happen to you. Eternal life means you not only belong to the family of God, but because Jesus died and then rose from the dead, overcoming death, you, too, will live forever.

Death is man's greatest enemy. It is man's greatest fear. But as a child of God, you no longer have to fear death. The grave may hold your body, but *you* will live on forever with Jesus Christ in Heaven. *"And this is what God has testified: He has given us eternal life, and this life is in His Son. So whoever has God's Son has life; whoever does not have His Son does not have life. I write this to you who believe in the Son of God, so that you may know you have eternal life"* (1 John 5:11-13).

FINALLY, you began the great adventure for which God created you.

Jesus said, *"My purpose is to give life in all its fullness"* (John 10:10). It's not just life after death which Jesus gives us. He also gives us full and abundant life here on earth. He gives us power for living—now!

"What this means is that those who become Christians become new persons. They are not the same anymore, for the old life is gone. A new life has begun!" (2 Corinthians 5:17). All the adventure of the universe is yours to experience, all the joy of being on the winning side, all the wisdom of God, all the peace of Heaven—it's all yours . . . and more . . . because of Jesus.

Now before we go on, let's pause and review those four laws that brought you into your new relationship with God. In fact, you might find it helpful to list these statements on cards and review them regularly—until you know them by heart. That way, when others start asking you what has brought about the marvelous changes they see in your life, you can share these same laws with them.

1. God loves you and offers a wonderful plan for your life.
2. People are sinful and separated from God. Therefore, they cannot have fellowship with God or receive God's full love.
3. Jesus Christ is the only way we can approach God. Through Jesus, you can experience God's love and His plan for your life.
4. Each person must receive Christ individually. It is not enough to belong to a church or have Christian parents. But if you receive Him, He will make you a "child of God" also.

HOW TO KNOW THAT CHRIST IS IN YOUR LIFE

People often ask, "How can I know for sure that I am a Christian—that Christ has come into my life?" Remember the promise we looked at in Revelation 3:20? Jesus says, ***"Look! Here I stand at the door and knock. If you hear Me calling and open the door, I will come in."*** You can know on the authority of the trustworthiness of God Himself and His Word that Christ has come into your life.

Thank God often that Christ is in your life and that He will never leave you. You can know that the living Christ indwells you and that you have eternal life, from the moment you invite Him in on the basis of His promise. He will not deceive you.

Can you think of anything more wonderful that could happen to you than receiving Christ? Before reading any further, why don't you close this book and thank God in prayer for what He has done for you. Remember, your relationship with God is not based on your "feelings." You may not feel any different now than you did before you prayed the prayer accepting Christ. The feelings will come later. Right now, accept your salvation by faith. Christ is Lord of your life because God said—in His Bible—that if you receive Him, Jesus will take control.

LIVING BY FAITH

The problem is that most of us don't really trust God to do what He says He will do in the Bible. The Bible says that *"a righteous person will live by faith"* (Hebrews 10:38) and that *"it is impossible to please God without faith"* (Hebrews 11:6). The object of our faith, then, is God Himself. Once we understand who God is—that He is not only holy and righteous, but He is loving and forgiving, all-wise and full of mercy—we should have no problem trusting Him.

God, the Bible says, loves us unconditionally. In other words, no matter what you do behind God's back—or to His face—He loves you. Once we understand that, we can ask His forgiveness and then trust Him with our lives totally and completely.

Many people are afraid of God. They see Him as some kind of "super fuzz," a huge cop sitting behind a cloud with a spiritual radar gun waiting to catch them disobeying the law so He can punish them. As a result, they are unwilling to totally surrender their life to Him for fear He'll slap them in leg irons and put them to work on the road gang. Better to stay as far away from God as possible, they feel.

Maybe you have felt this way about God. You felt if you gave your life to Jesus Christ that God would march you off to some concentration camp and beat the life out of you. Nothing is further from the truth. Instead of putting us in prison, faith in Christ sets us free.

I like the illustration used by Dr. Bill Bright, founder of Campus Crusade for Christ. Dr. Bright says: "My wife and I have two grown sons. Suppose that when they were little boys, they had come to greet me when I returned home from a trip and said, 'We love you. We missed you. We are so excited about your being home. We have been talking together and we have decided that we will do anything you want us to do. From now on, you issue the command and we will obey without any questions. We just want to please you.'

"What do you think," Dr. Bright asks, "would have been my attitude in response to their expression of love for me? If I had responded the way many people think God will respond if they said to Him, 'Lord, I'll do anything you want me to do and I'll go anywhere you want me to go,' I would have taken them by the shoulders, looked at them with an evil eye and said, 'I have just been waiting for you to say that. Now I'm going to make you regret your decision to trust as long as you live. I am going to take all the fun out of your lives. I will make you miserable as long as you live.'

"No, I wouldn't have said that. I would have put my arms around them and given them a big hug and said, 'Zac, Brad, I love you, too, and want to justify your faith in me. I want to be a better father to you. I want to do everything I can to help you find full meaningful lives.'"

Do you think God would do anything less for you? Remember, He loves you with an everlasting love. He sent His only Son to die for you and pay the penalty of your sin. No, He wants to bless you. He wants to give you power for living. But He cannot bless you unless you trust and obey Him—unless you are willing to live by faith.

As you exercise faith in an unlimited God and draw upon His unlimited resources, you will begin to experience the abundant life which Jesus came to give!

No, dear brothers and sisters, I am still not all
I should be, but I am focusing all my energies
on this one thing: Forgetting the past and
looking forward to what lies ahead,
I strain to reach the end of the race and
receive the prize for which God, through
Christ Jesus, is calling us up to heaven.

Philippians 3:13-14

HOW TO
KEEP ON GROWING

Becoming a Christian is only the beginning of a wonderful new life. God rarely takes people to heaven the moment they become Christians. He has work for you to do here on earth.

Being "born again" is like hatching out of an egg. Long before your birth, even before your conception, God had *you* in mind. All along, God has had a distinct purpose for you to fulfill on earth and in eternity. But you will never find or fulfill that wonderful purpose unless you grow as a Christian. Simply being hatched is not enough. You need to fly.

Søren Kierkegaard, the Danish philosopher, once told a story about a flock of barnyard geese in Denmark. Every Sunday the geese would gather in the barnyard near the feeding trough. One of their number, a "preaching goose," would struggle up onto the top rail of the fence and exhort the geese about the glories of goosedom. He would tell them how wonderful it was to be a goose rather than a chicken or a turkey. He would remind them of their great heritage and tell them of the marvelous possibilities in the future.

Occasionally, while he was preaching, a flock of wild geese, winging their way to sunny France, would fly overhead in a marvelous V-formation—thousands of feet in the air. When that happened, all the geese would excitedly look and say to one another, "That's who we really are. We are not destined to spend our lives in this stinking barnyard. Our destiny is to fly."

But then the wild geese would disappear from sight, their honking echoing across the horizon. The barnyard geese would look around at their comfortable surroundings, sigh, and return to the mud and filth of the barn.

They never did fly.

Sadly, there are a number of people in the Kingdom of God who remain in the barnyard, rather than spread their wings and learn to fly.

God has a purpose for YOU.

Salvation—in its highest sense—is the process of becoming who you really are in God's mind.

Conversion—being born again—is an event. It only happens once. It is the experience of moving from darkness to light, from death to life. Salvation, on the other hand, is a process. It begins at conversion and continues until you are fully transformed into the image of Jesus Christ.

MOVING ON FROM SPIRITUAL INFANCY

There are a number of things which keep us in the barnyard of infant Christianity, when God's highest purpose for us is to grow to flying maturity. It may be we're unwilling to run the risk of failure. Now that I'm a Christian, you might say, and I know I'm going to heaven, why do more?

Others are afraid to leave the comforts of the barnyard for the rugged life of faith. But anything worth having has its price. People who want to move on to spiritual maturity are willing to pay the price. These are the ones whom God uses in special ways to shape the world.

Paul told his friends at Philippi to *"put into action God's saving work in your lives, obeying God with deep reverence and fear. For God is working in you, giving you the desire to obey Him and the power to do what pleases Him"* (Philippians 2:12-13).

He was not talking about entering the Kingdom of God by good works. Remember, we read earlier that you do not work your way into the good graces of God. No, Paul was talking about the "process" of salvation whereby you grow in grace and are conformed to the image of God's Son, Jesus Christ. He was saying that growth as a Christian demands cooperation with God. In fact, he said you had to work at it. Then God, who works in you through His Holy Spirit, will make things happen.

In the next chapter Paul goes ahead and warns the church at Philippi against stopping along the way in their Christian life. He told them there was "more"—more than they had yet experienced in Christ. He was, in essence, telling them to grow as Christians.

"I am focusing all my energies on this one thing: Forgetting the past and looking forward to what lies ahead, I strain to reach the end of the race and receive the prize for which God, through Christ Jesus, is calling us up to heaven" (Philippians 3:13-14).

Paul constantly warned his friends of the danger of not growing. In fact, he went so far as to say he feared becoming "spiritually shipwrecked" if he failed to grow. *"Remember that in a race everyone runs, but only one person gets the prize. You also must run in such a way that you will win. All athletes practice strict self-control. They do it to win a prize that will fade away, but we do it for an eternal prize. So I run straight to the goal with purpose in every step. I am not like a boxer who misses his punches. I discipline my body like an athlete, training it to do what it should. Otherwise, I fear that after preaching to others I myself might be disqualified"* (1 Corinthians 9:24-27).

It sounds like Paul took this Christian life pretty seriously. He knew if he did not grow as a Christian, if he did not move forward, he could easily fall back into the old life. If this was such a major concern to a man like Paul, it seems the rest of us ought to take growth seriously as well.

The saddest of all people are those Christians who do not go on to full growth, who never leave the spiritual "nursery," who remain in diapers and booties rather than donning the gear of the mountain climber in order to scale the heights with the help of the Holy Spirit.

TOOLS TO ACCOMPLISH THE TASK

One of the purposes of this book is to give you the proper tools necessary to climb those magnificent mountains to spiritual maturity. Maybe a good way to understand these tools is by looking at the word *growth* in this acrostic:

G — Go to God in prayer daily (John 15:7).

R — Read God's Word daily (Acts 17:11).

O — Obey God, moment by moment (John 14:21).

W— Witness for Christ by your life and your words (Matthew 4:19).

T — Trust God for every detail of your life (1 Peter 5:7).

H — Holy Spirit—Allow God to control and empower your daily life (Galatians 5:16-17; Acts 1:8).

GO TO GOD IN PRAYER DAILY

Prayer is simply talking to God—and listening while God talks. It is the most basic expression of our faith. It is the "breathing" of our spiritual life. It is our lifeline to God.

Many people mistakenly think prayer needs to be formal—with "thees and thous." Not so. Prayer is nothing more than a child talking to his Daddy. It can be:

A cry for help in a time of need.

A squeal of delight for receiving a gift.

A plea in behalf of someone else.

A quiet time of adoration.

A period of listening as God talks.

A gentle time of receiving God's love.

Prayer is basically conversation with our Heavenly Father. For example:

"Forgive me, Father. I really blew it this time. I didn't want to explode at my son, but I did it anyway. Will You now give me strength to ask *his* forgiveness also?"

"Lord, remember last year when I began asking You for money to buy this new car. My faith wasn't very strong back then, was it? But oh, how I thank you for Your faithfulness. You provided. Now the car is ours. Thank You, thank You."

"Help me, God. I've been over this checkbook a dozen times and it still won't balance. Please show me where I made my mistake."

"O God, I'm not worthy to even talk to You. I've messed up my body with all these drugs; I've destroyed my loved ones . . . O God. . . . I need help. Please help me."

"Well, Lord, I've just signed the biggest contract of my life. Now I've got to produce. All I have is Yours; I'm just asking You to take over my brain so I can get the job done."

"Father, I've been battling this problem long enough. Now I'm going to turn it over to You and ask You to treat me as a little child until I learn my lesson."

Do you know any energetic, joyful Christians? You know, the kind who smile all the time, who seem to love everyone, who are on top of all their problems. Almost certainly, they know a secret: *prayer provides power for living.*

HOW DOES GOD ANSWER PRAYER?

Remember, God wants to grant your requests much more than the most loving father on earth wishes to give his children good things. But remember, too, He is your Father. As any good father, He knows how to give good gifts—and when to give them.

This means sometimes God says "No" to our requests. However, He never says "No" without having a better answer waiting for us just around the bend of the road.

It's important to remember this: When God says "No" to us, it's *not* because He can't afford it. Nor is it because He doesn't care. God is the owner of everything— riches, knowledge, wisdom, power, health, joy and love. Not only that, but He cares for us. He loves us more than any earthly father could ever love us. Thus, even though God does—on occasion—say "No," this is the exception. His usual response to us is "Yes!"

That's the reason, when we pray, we should *expect* a "Yes" answer.

When we know from the Bible what God's will is in a matter and act on that will even though we have yet to see it taking place in our lives, we open the door for God to answer our prayers even more quickly.

WRITE DOWN YOUR ANSWERS

I recommend you keep a prayer notebook. I have such a journal. It is just a little looseleaf notebook where I keep my prayer requests. On one page I write down my request. On the opposite page I note when and how God answered that request. As I look back over my notebook, I am amazed to discover that about 97% of my prayers of five years ago have been answered—and the rest are being answered.

I don't pray for everything every day. Some things I pray for only once a week—on specific days. But I keep my prayer journal just as faithfully as I brush my teeth. And I pray just as faithfully.

Writing down God's answers has encouraged me and given me more faith. Every year I pray for bigger and more "impossible" things. Each year God keeps increasing my faith—and my "bigger" prayers now are answered just as easily as my smaller prayers were answered a number of years ago. This is one of the joys of growth. You get to measure your own progress—especially in your prayer life.

What's the most important thing to remember about prayer? Just this. Jesus said, *"I am the way, the truth, and the life. No one can come to the Father except through Me"* (John 14:6). This means for prayer to be real prayer, it should be in the name of Jesus. When you come to God in the name of His Son, He pays attention.

READ GOD'S WORD DAILY

If prayer is your lifeline to God, then the Bible is the breadbasket. Just as it is important for you to develop good eating habits—eating regular meals of proper

Your word is a lamp
for my feet and a
light for my path.
Psalms 119:105

food—so it is vitally important for you to feast at God's table, the Bible, every day.

Bible reading, like prayer, can be made into a habit. A good habit. The Bible is absolutely central to our lives. There are several reasons for this.

First, the Bible, by the power of God's Spirit, produces faith in our hearts. Remember, we said salvation was a process of growth. One of the ways you can achieve your growth potential is through daily Bible reading. If you don't eat, your body won't grow. Likewise, if you don't read your Bible, you'll never grow beyond spiritual infancy.

Second, the Bible continues to nourish us throughout our lives. Jesus prayed that the Bible would have this effect upon His followers: **"Make them pure and holy by teaching them your words of truth"** (John 17:17).

How does God make us holy? By bringing us into regular contact with His Word. As we "eat" His Word, as we "digest" it, it goes into all our spiritual cells, and we become filled with the Word of God.

Third, the Bible is our standard for making decisions and forming opinions in every area of life. **"All Scripture is inspired by God and is useful to teach us what is true and to make us realize what is wrong in our lives. It straightens us out and teaches us to do what is right. It is God's way of preparing us in every way, fully equipped for every good thing God wants us to do"** (2 Timothy 3:16-17).

Someone said the definition of a Christian is one whose life is totally dominated and controlled by the Lord Jesus Christ. How do you know what Jesus wants of you? By reading His Word. In the pages of the Bible you will find God's will for your life.

I often drive from my home in Melbourne, on the east coast of Florida, to the central Florida city of Orlando—about 70 miles away—for editorial meetings with the staff of the magazine where I work as editor-at-large. We have an excellent Christian radio station in Melbourne, and I enjoy listening to music on my car radio. However, as I drive away from Melbourne I begin to lose the station on my radio. I can do a certain amount of fine tuning, but eventually the station disappears, and almost at once I pick up an Orlando station which plays music I don't care for. The station back in Melbourne is still broadcasting. My radio is still working. The trouble is I have moved too far away to get clear reception.

When I drive back home from Orlando at the close of the day, there is a spot along the highway where suddenly the Melbourne station is picked up. I'm back in range.

The reason I read my Bible daily is to keep me in range of God's voice. I make enough mistakes as it is without tuning out the Word of God from my life. A daily look at God's Word will give you access to God's wisdom and knowledge, keeping you safe from wrong decisions and filling you with power for living.

OBEY GOD, MOMENT BY MOMENT

How can you know if you really love Jesus—that it's not some kind of phony or artificial love? One of the most exciting things in the world is that God has given us a *standard* for love. Here it is.

"Those who obey My commandments are the ones who love Me. And because they love Me, My Father will love them, and I will love them. And I will reveal Myself to each one of them" (John 14:21).

How do we know we love Jesus? Because we obey His commands. Of course, we don't have to "prove" anything to anybody. But obedience becomes the gauge by which we can check ourselves. *"Love means doing what God has commanded us"* (2 John 6).

If you love God, the Bible says, you will also love others. *"And God Himself has commanded that we must love not only Him but our Christian brothers and sisters, too"* (1 John 4:21). That's pretty plain.

ARE YOU "IN CHRIST"?

The term "in Christ" is used 165 times in the New Testament. In fact, in the first chapter of Ephesians it is used nine times. That means being "in Christ" must be important. What does it mean?

You are IN CHRIST when you obey the still small voice of the Holy Spirit as He interprets the Bible. The Holy Spirit often speaks in a corrective voice. He is like those small rockets on the base of the giant rockets which carry the satellites into orbit. When the main rocket begins to veer off course, a command can be given from Mission Control which fires one of the small directional rockets. This pushes the spaceship back on course. The Holy Spirit often speaks to us like this. We sometimes call

Since God chose you to be the holy people whom He loves, you must clothe yourselves with tenderhearted mercy, kindness, humility, gentleness, and patience. You must make allowance for each other's faults and forgive the person who offends you. Remember, the Lord forgave you, so you must forgive others.

Colossians 3:12-13

it our "conscience," but for the Christian that is the voice of the Holy Spirit.

God does not bless disobedience. He may protect us while we are disobedient, but His blessings are reserved for those who obey Him. When we drive down the highway, my wife sometimes reminds me that the minute I exceed the speed limit I am "on my own" as far as God's blessings are concerned. He may protect me if I drive in disobedience to the law, but I have literally driven out from under His blessing—for God wants us to obey those civil laws which are not in direct conflict with the Bible.

Living a life of obedience to God—moment by moment—insures your growth as a Christian.

Likewise, we are told to love our brothers and sisters. Paul described this family as a "body." He pointed out the body has many parts: hands, feet, knees, elbows, ears, plus a lot of parts we can't see—things like liver, spleen and heart. Each one of us serves as part of that body. Just because you are a finger should not make you upset because someone else is an eye. You are both important, even though you have different functions to perform.

If the eye has picked up a grain of sand, it needs the finger to help it out. An elbow or a foot simply won't get the job done. Likewise, the finger needs the eye so it can "see" where the cotton swab is which will take the grain of sand out of the eye. And both need the feet to take them into the bathroom to find the cotton swab. Then, have you ever tried to put your finger to your eye with a stiff elbow? All parts are necessary to the body.

Loving one another means we are one body. That

body is called the church. It is not a building; it is not even an organization. It is a group of people—all different—who love the Lord and love each other. You need to be part of such a family if you are going to be obedient to God.

As you grow in your Christian life, remember the simple yet profound words of Jesus: *"If you love Me, obey My commandments"* (John 14:15).

WITNESS FOR CHRIST BY YOUR LIFE AND YOUR WORDS

Witnessing for Christ is simply being who you are. It does not mean that you need to preach; it doesn't necessarily mean you have to go door-to-door telling strangers about Jesus. All it means is living for Jesus every day so that not only your words tell of Christ, but your life reflects His life as well.

How do you witness with your life? By doing what we've just been discussing, obeying God's Word.

This doesn't mean you have to become a prude, wear strange clothes, or be unable to have a good time. It doesn't even mean you have to carry your Bible around all day either. It simply means you stay attached to Jesus at all times.

Jesus described it as branches attached to a vine. He is the vine. We are the branches. If we stay attached, we will bear fruit and our lives will be a testimony to all around us.

A Christian nurse in a psychiatric clinic had several opportunities to speak of her faith to doctors in the clinic. They all thought she was a little strange but didn't object too much since she was an excellent employee.

Then that woman's much-beloved teenage son was killed in a motorcycle accident. In the weeks that followed, one physician after another came to the nurse privately, admiring her faith and questioning her about the inner strength she showed. Her calm demeanor and peaceful spirit in the face of deep grief "preached a silent sermon" each finally was able to hear.

As a witness for Jesus you will affect the entire world. *"You are the light of the world,"* Jesus told his followers, *"like a city on a mountain, glowing in the night for all to see. Don't hide your light under a basket! Instead, put it on a stand and let it shine for all. In the same way, let your good deeds shine out for all to see, so that everyone will praise your heavenly Father"* (Matthew 5:14-16).

However, just being a witness with your life is not enough. Christian growth means you will also witness with your mouth. The redeemed of the Lord will "say so," says the psalmist. That means once you've been saved and filled with His Holy Spirit, you're going to want to tell others about this wonderful way of life. It will come as naturally as telling others about the person you love. Or about your new car. Or about your child or grandchild. God will give you just the right words—and will provide just the right people to talk to. All you have to do is make yourself available.

TRUST GOD FOR EVERY DETAIL OF YOUR LIFE

When God placed you into His family, He took responsibility for your life and all your problems. David said it better than anyone has ever said it: ***"The Lord is my shepherd; I have everything I need"*** (Psalms 23:1).

God is a God of unlimited resources. When you trust Him, you move beyond your understanding, beyond your comprehension, to a dimension of belief where you are willing to relax in life because you know there is a great, all-powerful, loving God watching over you. What, therefore, is there to fear?

How is this done?

When you reach the place that everything you own belongs to God, then everything God owns belongs to you.

It's that simple.

There are those who want to know God's will in advance so they may determine whether to do it or not. But God reveals His will only to those who are committed to follow it, regardless of what His will is.

Man's intellect is always trying to figure things out. He wants answers to all his "What if?" questions. God does not answer such questions, however. He simply says, "Trust me." That means God always reserves His best for those who leave the choices to Him. ***"Commit everything you do to the Lord. Trust Him, and He will help you"*** (Psalms 37:5).

For life consists of far more than food and clothing.
Look at the lilies and how they grow. They don't work
or make their clothing, yet Solomon in all his glory was
not dressed as beautifully as they are. And if God cares
so wonderfully for flowers that are here today and gone
tomorrow, won't He more surely care for you?
You have so little faith!

Luke 12:23, 27-28

HOLY SPIRIT—ALLOW GOD TO CONTROL AND EMPOWER YOUR DAILY LIFE

As a Christian, every day can be an exciting adventure. But in order for that to happen, you must be filled with the Holy Spirit. Far too many believers stop with the act of becoming a Christian and never move on to the victorious life of walking in the power of the Holy Spirit.

In fact, there is no single truth that is more important to the believer than being filled with the Holy Spirit. That is a powerful statement. And since it is true, you need to ask yourself: "How can I be filled with the Holy Spirit?"

But first, let's ask some other basic questions.

WHO IS THE HOLY SPIRIT?

Maybe it would be easier if I first told you who He is not. He is not an "it." Nor is He a ghost—some kind of shadowy vapor. (The word *ghost* in the King James Bible, by the way, is the ancient translation of the word better translated *spirit.*) The Holy Spirit is not some weird, ethereal, mystical feeling or impersonal presence.

The Holy Spirit is the third person of the Trinity: Father, Son, and Holy Spirit. He is a real person. He has a personality. He has feelings. He may be hurt, grieved, loved, honored, known, and communicated with. He has infinite intellect, will, and emotion. He possesses all the divine nature of God. He is equal in every way with God the Father and God the Son. And—this is most important—He is waiting to take control of your life.

WHY DID THE HOLY SPIRIT COME?

Before Jesus left earth following His resurrection, He called his followers together and told them that when He returned to Heaven He would send the Holy Spirit back to earth. The Holy Spirit would actually live inside every believer! In fact, the very same power that raised Christ from the dead could then control the life of every Christian.

The Holy Spirit's ministry in a believer's life takes on many forms.

For one, He convicts us of our sin. Remember, He is a *Holy* Spirit. That means He is pure. When He fills us, He does so to purify us—to make us holy.

He also takes away our doubts—those pestering questions about our salvation. He convinces us we really are the children of God—just as the Bible says.

The Holy Spirit makes the presence of Jesus real in us. When Jesus was on earth, He spent a great deal of time with His disciples. He taught them and answered their questions. He was their most intimate friend. It's no wonder they grieved so deeply when He left them.

It was to them Jesus said, *"I will ask the Father, and He will give you another Counselor, who will never leave you. He is the Holy Spirit, who leads into all truth"* (John 14:16-17). He arrived, just as Jesus promised, and has been with us ever since, making Jesus as real to every Christian as if He were still here in the flesh.

The Holy Spirit does many other things.

He teaches us.

He helps us when we don't know how to pray—actually praying through us. *"The Holy Spirit helps us in our distress. For we don't even know what we should pray for, nor how we should pray. But the Holy Spirit prays for us with groanings that cannot be expressed in words"* (Romans 8:26).

He gives us power—supernatural power. In fact, Jesus told his disciples, *"When the Holy Spirit has come upon you, you will receive power"* (Acts 1:8). Power for what? Well, for many things—but primarily to be witnesses of Jesus. Filled with the Holy Spirit, those disciples were transformed from a cowardly and defeated band of leaderless stragglers to a bold army of spiritual warriors who challenged and defeated the forces of hell which held the world in bondage.

But perhaps the most wonderful thing the Holy Spirit does is to produce in you the life of Jesus. When the Holy Spirit is allowed to take control of your life, then Jesus in all His character and personality is at home in you. He will love and live through you. You will begin to see in your life what the Bible (in Galatians 5:22) calls the "fruit of the Spirit": love, joy, peace, patience, kindness, goodness, faithfulness, gentleness, and self-control. It won't happen all at once, for no tree bears fruit overnight. But day by day you will see your life changing as you take on the character of Jesus. That's exciting!

WHAT DOES IT MEAN TO BE FILLED
WITH THE HOLY SPIRIT?

At the very moment you were born again, the Holy Spirit took up residence in your life. However, that does not mean you are "filled" with the Holy Spirit. To be filled means you are controlled and empowered. It means you are relying on the power of God to change your life, rather than trying to do it yourself. Power for living is yours only when you yield to Him and let Him control your life. You cannot live the Christian life in your own power through self-determination and self-discipline. Only Jesus was able to live a perfect life; only as He lives in you—through His Spirit—can you live victoriously.

In a nutshell, to be filled with the Holy Spirit means to be filled with Jesus.

HOW CAN I BE FILLED WITH THE HOLY SPIRIT?

Several years ago I visited one of those huge hydro-electric dams on the Columbia River in Washington State. I had heard of such things as turbines and generators but for some reason had always thought the power from those dams was provided by the water which roared over the spillway. It never occurred to me—a flatlander from Florida—that the real power was not in the froth which splattered over the top, but was produced in the machines hidden far below the top of the dam.

We took an elevator deep into the mysterious interior of the dam. Stepping out into a huge room as long as the dam was wide, I was suddenly in the middle of more power than I had ever imagined possible. The spotless room, with the huge cranes overhead on their tracks, was filled with a deep *huummm*. The very air was vibrating with power. Where did it come from? Not from the water which splashed over the spillway hundreds of feet above. Nor did it come from those giant, hidden turbines in the floor. It came from the millions of pounds of water pressure in the lake above. As the water moved through those slow-turning turbines, it created enough power to provide electricity for half the state of Washington and part of Oregon.

So does the Holy Spirit move through the spiritual turbine of the believer, creating incredible power.

Being filled with the Holy Spirit involves a complete surrender of your will, without reservation, to the will of God. This is not an event—it is a process, a continual process. Paul wrote to his friends in Ephesus and told them to *"let the Holy Spirit fill and control you"* (Ephesians 5:18). His language means to be continually filled. What he is saying is, "be filled, and filled, and filled, and filled with the Holy Spirit."

Why do we need to keep on being filled with the Holy Spirit? Well, for one thing, we often take back the control of our lives that we had already yielded to Him. We decide that we want to be our own master and make our own decisions. When we do, the Holy Spirit is saddened—that is, the flow of His power through us is hindered. In order to get this power restored, we must agree with God that we have sinned and once again yield the control of our lives to His Spirit.

This experience is often referred to as "spiritual breathing." While a baby takes its first breath shortly after it is born, unless it keeps on breathing, it will die. Likewise, Paul tells us to be filled *continually* with the Holy Spirit. Spiritual breathing means you exhale anything which hinders or "grieves" the Holy Spirit, and you continually inhale the power of the Holy Spirit. As you exhale impure air, you then inhale pure air.

If you want to be filled with the Holy Spirit, you need to exhale the impurities of sin in your life. This is known as confession—agreeing with God that you have sinned, that you have been in control of some area of your life and you are now exhaling that impurity. Then immediately thank God for forgiving your sin, and once again surrender the control of your life to Him.

You will want to make "spiritual breathing" a consistent part of your life, so that you can live each day filled with the wonderful power of the Holy Spirit.

It is possible that up until this moment, the Holy Spirit has been just a "guest" in your life. (Remember that He came to live in you the moment you became a Christian.) But He wants to be more than a guest. He wants to be the Master of your home. He wants complete access to the library of your mind, the dining room of your social life. He wants to be invited into the small, hidden rooms where you previously engaged in shameful activity. In short, He wants to be in charge of your life.

That sounds like a pretty major surrender. And it is! But in exchange for surrendering your life to Him, the Holy Spirit fills you with the supernatural power over sin; an abundant, meaningful life; and the indescribable love, joy, peace, patience, and goodness of Jesus Himself.

Like your salvation, the filling of the Holy Spirit is a gift from God. You cannot earn either. Both are received by faith and the complete yielding of your will to Him.

Do you want to be filled with the Holy Spirit? You don't have to search for Him—or wait for Him. He is already dwelling in you, waiting for you to allow Him to control your life. If this is the desire of your heart, then simply tell God that you want to be filled with the Holy Spirit, accept His power by faith, and begin to thank Him. All the power of Heaven is yours as you begin living the Spirit-filled life.

FELLOWSHIP AND THE CHURCH

One of the most practical helps in our growth as Christians is our meeting (fellowshipping) with other believers in Christ. Fellowship is spending time and doing things with others who love Jesus Christ.

In a fireplace several logs burn brightly together, but place one alone on the cold hearth and the fire goes out. Christians need to be together, or the fire of enthusiasm will go out. That relationship is vital for Christian growth. God's Word tells us in Hebrews 10:25 to *"let us not neglect our meeting together."*

The best place to find this fellowship with other Christians is in a church in your area. It is also here that you will receive good teaching from the Word of God and experience the joy of worshipping Him.

As you consider a church you might want to be a part of, let me suggest four questions that you might ask to help you in evaluating which would be the best one for you:

1. How does the church treat God's Word, the Bible? Does it recognize the Bible as coming from God and teach it as such?

2. How does the church treat the Son of God? Does it recognize Jesus Christ as God's sinless Son who died on the cross for our sins and was resurrected from the dead?

3. How does the church treat God the Father? Does it recognize Him as loving and merciful, yet a just and righteous Father, who is worthy of our adoration and worship?

4. How do the people in this church treat one another? Are they kind and loving individuals who obviously care for each other and desire to help and encourage each other in walking with God?

Ask God to help you find a local church for weekly fellowship and worship.

There you have it: GROWTH. Like children, we are afraid to face it, but when it comes we think it's great. So your growth as a Christian will be both exciting—and useful.

By way of review we see that to move on from our initial conversion to spiritual maturity, we need to use these special "tools":

G — Go to God in prayer daily.
R — Read God's Word daily.
O — Obey God, moment by moment.
W— Witness for Christ by your life and your words.
T — Trust God for every detail of your life.
H — Holy Spirit—Allow God to control and
empower your daily life.

Your Christian growth gives glory to God and allows Him to bless you with His Presence—and that Presence brings power for living.

Forever, O Lord, Your word stands
firm in heaven. Your faithfulness extends
to every generation, as enduring
as the earth You created.

Psalms 119:89-90

WHAT THE BIBLE IS ALL ABOUT

The Greek philosopher, Plato, once said there are three valid sources of knowledge:

1. The five senses—touch, taste, smell, sight, sound—which we share with the animal kingdom.

2. Reason—which sets man apart from the lower animals.

3. The third he called "Divine Madness"—by which he referred to the spiritual world of supernatural communication.

Later his disciple, Aristotle, eliminated the third source—the entire intuitive faculty by which divine perception comes to man. Aristotle said knowledge comes only through the five senses and reason.

Much of the Western world was affected by what Aristotle taught. But in Eastern and primitive cultures, references to the spirit world—the world of dreams, visions and supernatural communication—are common in all walks of life.

While Aristotle would have rejected the Bible as a source of knowledge, Jesus never hesitated when He said the Bible is the primary way through which God reveals Himself to mankind.

Now, 2,000 years later, more and more people are seeing that Jesus is right. Voltaire, the famous French atheist (who was a follower of Aristotle rather than Jesus), died in 1778. Before dying, he said the Bible and Christian faith would not be believed in one hundred years. On the one hundredth anniversary of his statement, the Geneva Bible Society purchased Voltaire's printing press and house and started to print Bibles from there.

Two hundred six years after Voltaire, the president of the United States declared the year 1983 as "The Year of the Bible." Why would the president of the greatest nation in history proclaim the Bible as mankind's greatest source of knowledge?

Millions of people are looking for a reliable voice of authority. They have found they cannot trust treaties between nations; they cannot trust the statements of scientists; even the great religious leaders are often wrong. The Bible—the Word of God—is the only real authority we have. Proven across the years, the Bible sheds light on human nature, world problems and human suffering. But beyond that, it clearly reveals *the way to God.*

The Bible is God revealing Himself to mankind.

Billy Graham is right when he says of the Bible: "The Bible is old; yet it is ever new. It is the most modern book in the world today. There is a false notion that a book as ancient as the Bible cannot speak to the needs of modern man. Men somehow think that in an age of

The earth is the Lord's, and everything in it.
The world and all its people belong to Him.
For He laid the earth's foundation on the seas
and built it on the ocean depths.

Psalms 24:1-2

scientific achievement, when knowledge has increased more in the past 25 years than in all preceding centuries put together, this ancient book is out of date. But to all who read and love the Bible, it is relevant for our generation.

"It is in the Holy Scriptures that we find the answers to life's ultimate questions: Where did I come from? Why am I here? Where am I going? What is the purpose of my existence?"

The word *bible* comes from the Greek word *biblios,* meaning "book." But the Bible is more than a book—or a collection of books. It is God's written revelation of His will to men. Behind and beneath this book, above and beyond this book, is the God of the book. For the Bible is all about God—and especially it is about God's Son, Jesus Christ.

MORE THAN A BOOK

The Bible contains 66 books, written by 40 authors, covering a period of approximately 1,600 years. These authors came from all walks of life and include kings, peasants, prophets, poets, fishermen, statesmen, scholars, a businessman, a doctor and a missionary. It is separated into two major sections, the dividing place being the birth of Jesus Christ.

The first section is called the Old Testament. This portion was written mostly in Hebrew (with the exception of a few short passages in Aramaic) and was completed almost 400 years prior to the birth of Christ. The New

Testament was written in the Greek language. Our present-day English Bibles are all translated from these original languages.

The word *testament* actually means "covenant," or "agreement." The Old Testament is a record of God's covenants with man—and points toward the coming of God's Son, Jesus. The New Testament is the record of the fulfillment of that covenant agreement through Jesus Christ.

WHO IT IS ABOUT

In the sign language for the deaf, the sign for Jesus is to point to the palm of each hand with the index finger of the other hand. This is symbolic of the nail prints in the hands of Jesus.

The sign for the Bible is to point with first one index finger, then the other, to the palm of each hand, then to open the palms up as if they were a book. In other words, the Bible is a book about Jesus Christ.

Several years ago I was visiting in Hong Kong and rode the hydrofoil from Hong Kong across the harbor to the tiny Portuguese colony of Macao. There, on a hill overlooking the harbor of Macao, the Portuguese once built a massive cathedral. Several centuries ago a typhoon proved stronger than the work of men's hands, and the huge, stone building fell in ruins. However, the front wall of the old cathedral still stands, with its wide steps leading down to the ancient cobblestone street bordering the harbor. High on top of that jutting wall, challenging the elements down through the years, is a great bronze cross.

In 1825 Sir John Bowering sailed his ship into Hong Kong harbor and caught a glimpse of that great cross, towering above the ruins of the old Cathedral of St. Paul. Sir John was deeply moved. Retiring to the cabin of his ship, picking up a quill, he dipped it in ink and wrote these words in his journal:

> In the cross of Christ I glory
> Towering o'er the wrecks of time.
> All the light of sacred story
> Gathers round its head sublime.

The central message of the Bible is the cross of Jesus Christ. Every book of the Bible either points forward to the coming of Jesus, or points backward toward His work on Calvary.

There is a marvelous story in the book of Luke about an event that took place eight days after Jesus was born. His mother, Mary, and Joseph had taken the tiny baby to the Temple in Jerusalem so He could be circumcised according to the Jewish law. When they entered the Temple, they were spotted by an old rabbi, a Godly man named Simeon, who had been studying the Old Testament all his life. By reading the Old Testament writings he had become convinced that the central message of the Old Testament was to point toward the coming of the Messiah—God's Son. In fact, the Holy Spirit had told him he would not die until he had seen the Saviour with his own eyes.

That day, when Mary and Joseph entered the Temple court carrying their tiny Baby, something sparked in the old man's heart. He rushed forward, tears in his eyes, and asked Mary if he could hold the Baby for just a moment. Taking the tiny Child in his arms, he gazed down on the face of Jesus. Then, turning his face heavenward, he prayed:

"Lord, now I can die in peace! As You promised me, I have seen the Savior You have given to all people. He is a light to reveal God to the nations, and He is the glory of Your people Israel!" (Luke 2:29-32).

Then Simeon said something very significant. *"This Child will be rejected by many in Israel, and it will be their undoing. But He will be the greatest joy to many others. Thus, the deepest thoughts of many hearts will be revealed."* Then looking deep into the tender eyes of the young mother, the old man said, *"And a sword will pierce your very soul"* (Luke 2:34-35).

Simeon was referring to the messianic prophecies he had been reading in the Old Testament—the prophecies which foretold the coming of the Son of God. In particular he was referring to a prophecy in Genesis when God said to the serpent, Satan, in the Garden of Eden, *"From now on, you and the woman will be enemies, and your offspring and her offspring will be enemies. He will crush your head, and you will strike his heel"* (Genesis 3:15). Simeon also made reference to a prophecy by Isaiah, 700 years before the birth of Jesus Christ: *"I will make You a light to the Gentiles, and You will bring My salvation to the ends of the earth"* (Isaiah 49:6).

This is what the Lord says:
"Let not the wise man gloat in his wisdom,
or the mighty man in his might, or the rich
man in his riches. Let them boast in this alone:
that they truly know Me and understand
that I am the Lord who is just and righteous,
Whose love is unfailing, and that I delight
in these things. I, the Lord, have spoken!"

Jeremiah 9:23-24

GOD'S DREAM

From the very beginning, God had a dream. The dream was for man to be restored into full fellowship with God. Jesus was the answer to that dream. All the Godly men across the ages who wrote the Bible picked up snatches of that dream—and included them in their writings. Therefore, throughout the Bible—from the time of Creation until the birth of Christ—you find the biblical writers referring to this messianic dream. Jesus, then, is the central theme of the Bible.

Abraham saw His reflection in Melchizedek, king of Salem.

Jacob called Him Shiloh.

To Moses He was the Passover Lamb and the Lifted-Up One.

To Joshua He was Captain of our Salvation.

Ruth saw Him as Family Redeemer.

Samuel portrayed Him as our King.

David called Him Lion of Judah and Good Shepherd.

To Solomon He was the Beloved.

Ezra and Nehemiah pictured Him as our Restorer.

To Esther He was our Advocate.

Job said He was my Redeemer.

Isaiah described Him as a Suffering Servant.

Jeremiah saw Him at the Potter's wheel.

Ezekiel called Him the Son of Man.

Daniel called Him the Prince and the Smiting Stone.

Hosea likened Him to a Bridegroom redeeming a fallen wife.

To Joel He was the Restorer.

Amos saw Him as a Heavenly Husbandman.

To Obadiah He was Saviour.

Jonah saw Him as Resurrection and Life.

Micah called Him a Witness.

To Nahum He was a Stronghold in a day of trouble.

Habakkuk described Him as God of my Salvation.

To Zephaniah He was a Jealous Lord.

Haggai said He was the Desire of All Nations.

Zechariah called Him the Righteous Branch.

Malachi declared Him the Sun of Righteousness.

And John the Baptist cried out: *"Look! There is the Lamb of God who takes away the sin of the world!"* (John 1:29).

As you read through the Old Testament, there looms on the horizon of history One Person through whom God would establish His Kingdom on earth: Jesus Christ. Micah said He would be born in Bethlehem. Isaiah said He would be born of a virgin and would be called Emmanuel. David and Isaiah told how He would die, and Job prophesied of His resurrection. Others pointed out He would be introduced by a strange prophet like Elijah, that He would work miracles, speak in parables, be rejected by leaders, be a Smitten Shepherd, a Man of Sorrows, would enter Jerusalem riding on a colt, would be betrayed by a friend for 30 pieces of silver and would be led as a lamb to the slaughter. He would die with the wicked. His hands and feet would be pierced. Not a bone of His body would be broken. Lots would be cast for His garments. He would be in a tomb three days, would rise from the dead and would ascend to Heaven at God's right hand.

It was foretold by David, Isaiah, Daniel, and Jeremiah that the Messiah would offer a new covenant for His people. He would send the Holy Spirit. His Kingdom would be of the Gentiles and would be universal and endless.

All of this was written hundreds of years before Christ's birth, at which time the angels appeared to the shepherds on the hillside, saying they had good tidings of great joy.

THE MIRACLE OF COMPOSITION

Suppose one man from each nation in the earth were to work a lifetime, carving a tiny piece of marble. One day, all these men, none of whom had ever met or even known anyone else was carving marble, would all gather in a small village in the hills south of Jerusalem—each one bringing their tiny piece of marble with them. The man who had carved what looked like big toes would place his little pieces on the ground. Then the man who had carved the feet without toes or heels would attach his pieces—and they would fit perfectly. More toes would be added, each just the right size and shape. Then the man with the heels would attach his pieces. Then the ankles, the legs, the knees—each piece fitting so perfectly not even a seam showed—until the entire statue was complete, perfect in every detail.

How could such a statue be accounted for unless there was someone with a blueprint who had outlined to each man exactly what he was to carve?

No wonder the angels sang of "good tidings and great joy." The Miracle of the Ages, the One the Bible is all about, had been born in Bethlehem!

Remember, God's Word is the foundation of all we know about God—and of His plan for mankind. It tells of the origin of sin and how it separated man from God. Even though the Bible contains the Law of God given to Moses on Mt. Sinai, we also discover how utterly impossible it is for the law to bring man the salvation he needs. Thus we find in its pages that the one purpose of God is to prepare the way for the coming of the Redeemer of the World, Jesus Christ.

Although the Bible is a library of books, it is also "the Book." It is a story, a grand story, of God's love for His people and the price He was willing to pay to restore us into perfect fellowship with Him. While it is divine, it is also human. The thought is divine; the expression of the communication is human.

So here we have a book unlike all others. The Book, a divine revelation, a revelation of God to man communicated through men, that moves on smoothly from its beginning to its great end. Behind each event stands God, the builder of history, the maker of the ages. Eternity bounds the one side, eternity bounds the other side, and time is in between. You can study the minutest detail everywhere and see that there is one great purpose down through the ages—the eternal design of our Mighty God to redeem a wrecked world and give each of us—you and me—power for living.

The Old Testament is the account of God dealing with a nation—the Israelites. The New Testament is an account of God dealing with a Man—His Son. The nation was founded in order to bring the Man into the world.

God became Man in the presence of His Son so we might know what God is like. If you want to know what God is like, look at Jesus, for He is the perfect revelation of God.

His appearance on earth still marks the central event of all history. Even today's calendars are dated from that special time. The Old Testament set the stage. The New Testament describes the play.

And what a marvelous play it is. God is the author. Jesus Christ is the central character. The Holy Spirit is the power behind each of the characters—including the Son of God.

Jesus was a perfect man. He was kind, tender, gentle, patient and full of love. He worked miracles to feed the hungry, heal the sick, and raise the dead. Multitudes came to Him and He taught them about the Kingdom of God. But He threatened the religious people of the day—eventually they killed Him. Yet even this had been foretold. It was necessary; for Jesus became the perfect sacrifice for our sins. By His atoning death the way was opened for all people to once again have fellowship with the Father.

Then, the greatest of all miracles—Jesus rose from the dead! He is alive today. He is not merely an historical figure, but a living Person—the most important fact of history, and the most vital force in the world.

His friends and followers wanted Him to remain on earth after His resurrection from the dead. But He said He had to leave. He had to leave so He could send His Holy Spirit. That Spirit, He said, the same Spirit who gave Him power to rise from the dead, would come and fill each Christian from that time on—giving them power for living.

Several years ago I spent time with a young woman who had been part of the Charles Manson gang. She had been convicted on seven counts of first-degree murder and sentenced to die in the California gas chamber. Shortly before she was to be executed, her sentence was changed to life in prison. During that time she received Jesus Christ as her Lord and Saviour. She subsequently led a number of young women in prison into a salvation experience with Jesus Christ.

When I heard about this, I sought and received permission to visit her in her cell at the California Institution for Women near Chino. We became good friends during these visits.

On one of these visits she told me how she had received Christ. The first week after she arrived in prison, she received a Bible through the mail. She tossed it to one side and didn't even look at it for more than a year. But unknown to her, a large number of people were praying for her. She received several letters from strangers, telling her about God's forgiving love. Then one day she took the Bible off the shelf in her little cell, brushed the dust off the cover, and settled back to read. Knowing virtually nothing about the Bible (although she had attended Sunday school as a child), she began to read—starting with the first page.

It was tough reading, but she was determined to find out what the Bible was all about. When she got to the book of Exodus and read the story of the Children of Israel, she became angry. Here was the story of God's love and provision. He delivered the Israelites from captivity in Egypt, opened the sea so they could escape, protected them from harm, provided water from rocks and manna every morning. Still the people griped and complained. Why, she asked herself, would anyone who was loved as much as God loved the Israelites refuse that love and respond so selfishly?

She read on through the Psalms—those beautiful love songs by David. Time after time she had to put the Bible down because tears filled her eyes. All she had ever known from childhood was hate. That was why she joined the Manson gang and participated in those horrible murders. Now she was reading about a tender, loving Heavenly Father. She had never known such love existed.

The books by the prophets all told her of a Saviour— one who would take away her sin and give her power for living. But they didn't tell her how to find Him—just that He was coming.

In the Gospels she read the life story of Jesus. He was all she imagined Him to be—loving, tender, kind, yet a man of justice and righteousness. It was what she had longed for all her life. She read on through the book of Acts and saw how those early Christians, full of the Holy Spirit, had gone out and performed the same miracles Jesus performed. How she longed for that same power in her life. It wasn't until she finally reached the last book in the Bible that she discovered how she could be forgiven of her sins and receive power for living.

Reading through the book of Revelation, she came upon the words of Jesus, an invitation she sensed was given just to her.

"I am the One who corrects and disciplines everyone I love. Be diligent and turn from your indifference" (Revelation 3:19).

She paused in her reading, letting the words sink in. Could it be she was in prison not because she was a murderer, but because God loved her and was waiting for her to repent so He could give her power for living?

She read on. *"Look! Here I stand at the door and knock. If you hear Me calling and open the door, I will come in, and we will share a meal as friends. I will invite everyone who is victorious to sit with Me on My throne, just as I was victorious and sat with My Father on His throne"* (Revelation 3:20-21).

With tears streaming down her face, she slipped off her cot in her lonely prison cell and knelt on the concrete floor. The Son of God was knocking at the door of her heart, asking to come in. Even though she was a murderer, He was waiting for her to repent and ask His forgiveness. She opened the door of her heart and prayed a simple prayer. "Come in, Lord Jesus, take over my life."

Susan Atkins is still in prison, but she is a free woman. She has been set free by the Son of God. She has found new life right where she is—and she has received power to live that life through Jesus Christ.

The Bible, to Susan Atkins, was more than an ancient book. It was—and is—the Book of Life.

But they delight in doing everything the Lord wants; day and night they think about His law. They are like trees planted along the riverbank, bearing fruit each season without fail. Their leaves never wither, and in all they do, they prosper.

Psalms 1:2-3

MAKING THE BIBLE A PART OF YOUR LIFE

Suppose you are planning a trip. You carefully pack your suitcase, perhaps suspend your newspaper delivery, even get your car checked and gather your family to go with you. You attend to every necessary detail except one: you never pick up a road map.

Because you're in a hurry to reach your destination, you jump in your car and start driving. Which direction do you go: north, east, south or west? Does it make any difference?

Since you feel you're headed the right way, you keep on driving. You are like the bus driver who, after a day of hard driving, turned to his passengers and said, "Folks, I have good news and bad news.

"The bad news is we're lost and I haven't the faintest idea where we are. The good news is we're making excellent time!"

A lot of people start out on their Christian journey this way. They are so excited about their progress they get lost along the way. They are so intent on reaching their destination they ignore the basic steps they should take to get there. In other words, they ignore the fundamental Instruction Manual, the Word of God, which has the principles by which we live and die.

In this chapter I want to give you some practical, helpful hints on Bible study—which will make the journey much easier.

WHERE DO YOU START?

First, everything you need to know about power for living is found in the Bible. In its pages are God's instructions on how to raise your family, how to treat your wife or husband, how you should eat, how you should worship . . . in short, everything you need to know about money, work, fear, pain, sex, and death. Any problem you can experience has its solution in the Bible.

Start by recognizing that even though the Bible is an entire library of 66 books—it is also one book. In Genesis you find the beginnings; in Revelation you discover how it all winds up. And from Exodus (the second book) to Jude (the next-to-last book) you see how God carried out His purpose. You cannot dispense with any part of it.

The Old Testament is the foundation; the New Testament is the superstructure. A foundation is of no value unless a building is built upon it. A building is impossible unless there is a foundation—and makes no sense unless there is a superstructure. Thus both Old and New Testaments are of equal value.

The Bible is one book, one history, one story. His story. Behind every event stands God, the builder of history, the maker of the ages. In its original version the books of the Bible were not divided into chapters and verses. Each book was written to be read from beginning to end. God took great pains to give it to us as a progressive revelation of Himself, and you should take great pains to read it from beginning to end. You'll never understand it if you simply open it at random and begin reading.

This does not mean, however, that particular verses or chapters will not become especially meaningful to you. History is filled with stories of men and women who simply opened the Bible, and heard God speaking so profoundly it changed their lives. In the beginning, it may be too difficult to wade through long books and chapters. Verses and sections of verses, especially Psalms and Proverbs, will be meaningful to you regardless of the order in which you read them. But this should never be enough for earnest and systematic study of the Bible as a complete unity. Just as you would never dream of going to the library, checking out a book, and begin reading in the middle, so you need to learn to view the Bible as one book.

A LOVE STORY

The Bible is the greatest love story ever written. It is the story of God's love for all mankind—especially you. It is not a book of verses such as you would find on greeting cards; it is a revelation. It must be read, digested, studied, questioned and revered from beginning to end. Don't divide it into short devotional paragraphs and think you can understand its message. Come to its pages with common sense, believe that every book is about something, and read and reread until you find out what that book is about.

Since the Bible was inspired by the Holy Spirit, you need the Holy Spirit's power to help you understand it, to interpret it. That is one of the functions of the Holy Spirit—to help you understand the Bible. Therefore, before you begin any serious study of the Bible, ask the Holy Spirit to fill you. Only as He interprets it to you will it make any sense. Otherwise it will be nothing more than great literature, interesting history, or a jumble of words and genealogies.

Are all the books of the Bible of equal importance? No, but all are indispensable. If you were to ask me if my brain is more important than my hand, I would tell you my brain is more important. Yet my hand is important also—and I would have a difficult time without it. So with the Bible. Every book is necessary to make a perfect whole, but some portions are more precious than others. You can't take away the books of Esther or Song of Songs and have a perfect revelation of God. Yet no one says either of these two books is comparable with the Gospel of John or the book of Exodus. All are part of an organism, and that organism is not complete if any part is missing.

THE ABC'S OF BIBLE READING

How, then, should we begin reading? Why not begin reading the same way you would visit an art museum. Walk with your guide down the long rows of pictures. What do you do? Well, for one thing, you don't walk hurriedly. Nor do you carry on a conversation about the stock market or the baseball World Series with a friend. You listen carefully to your guide as he pauses in front of each picture. There he describes, not the picture, but the artist. He tells you who the artist was, what he was going through when he painted the picture, where he lived and what he was trying to express through his art. Then he talks about various art forms. Some paintings are realistic; others are abstract. You need to understand the artist's techniques and style, how he used composition, lights, color, shadows and proportions. Then, finally, the guide will ask you to study the painting itself and see if it has a message for you as an individual.

That's the way you should study the Bible.

Begin with the Author

Studying the Bible is much like learning to interpret art. First, you should know the author of each book. As a writer I have learned, for instance, that those who understand my books best are those who know me. The better you know me, the better you will understand what I have written.

That's the reason you need to start with the Holy Spirit when studying the Bible. The Holy Spirit worked through every writer of these books, revealing the nature of God.

Then you need to learn as much as you can about the human writers. Amos, for instance, wrote the book that carries his name. It is helpful to know that Amos was a farmer, a herdsman, that he lived in a time when the Kingdom of Israel was divided into two nations—a southern and a northern kingdom, much like the United States was divided during the Civil War. Amos lived in the southern kingdom called Judah. When he prophesied against the northern kingdom, he got a lot of support from his southern audience. But when he began pointing out the sins of Judah, they ran him out of town. Knowing this background helps in understanding the content of the book.

Take another case. It is helpful to know that the same man who wrote the Gospel of Luke also wrote the book of Acts. His name was Luke. He was a physician turned biographer. Not only did he write one of the four biographies of Jesus found in the New Testament, but he later traveled with the Apostle Paul and wrote the history of the early church—actually the biography of Paul in a book called Acts. When you discover that Luke was a medical doctor, you can understand why he uses certain words, his close attention to detail, and his many references to physical healing and miracles.

Each writer of the Bible—from Moses to the Apostle John—used a different style. But each was inspired by the Holy Spirit, and all he wrote was true and without error. No one writer had a full picture of God, but when their writings are put together you see God in all His glory—in His entirety.

Read for the Big Picture

A good practice is to train yourself to read the Bible one book at a time. The first time you read a book in the Bible, try to get an overall feel for what the book says. This is the skyscraper view. Don't worry about details; try to get the panoramic sweep. It's like climbing into a tree to see everything from above.

Start, for instance, with the book of Mark. Mark is easy to read. It is an action book about the life of Jesus, full of stories without too much difficult teaching.

Or you may want to start with Genesis. It's the same kind of book, filled with wonderful history. That is, I like to see it as a book of biographies of men like myself. So I read about Adam and Eve. Then about Noah. There is a long section about Abraham. Another about Isaac. And finally those thrilling stories about Jacob—who was a man so much like I am. When you view Genesis as a book of stories about people, it is not only easy, but exciting to read.

Do not start in the middle of the Bible with books like Daniel or Isaiah. They simply won't make sense until you begin to get the big picture.

Read for Details

Don't stop with first impressions. Now that you are looking at the Bible from the top of a skyscraper, move on down and get a sidewalk perspective as well. At this point it helps to begin to follow some steps.

(1) *Start by reading a book a week.* This is not as diffi-cult as it sounds. The longest book in the Bible can be read by spending less than one hour a day. Simply divide the book into seven equal parts, set aside a special time each day to read, and establish a habit of Bible reading.

(2) *Use a notebook.* Don't just read. Make notes as you do. Underline passages in your Bible that seem signifi-cant to you and make notes in your notebook about any questions you may have, or any ideas that the Holy Spirit may give you as you read.

I often use my notebook during Bible reading as I do when I pray. I make notes on what God is saying to *me.* After all, that's why we should be reading the Bible. It is more than God's Word. It is God's Word to ME. Well, if God is speaking to me, I'd better take notes on what He is saying. So I nearly always read the Bible with an open notebook— pen ready to jot down God's personal message to me.

Perhaps the most meaningful Bible I have is the one my father used immediately after he received Jesus Christ as his personal Saviour and Lord at the age of 62. My father had always been a good man—an active member of the church. But it wasn't until he went through a deep, per-sonal trauma that he surrendered his life to Jesus Christ. Immediately he began an intense study of the Bible. He wanted to know what God was saying to him. He began by using a modern translation. Not only did he read, but he underlined, using different colors for different emphasis, and he made many notes in the margins of the Bible. It is these notes, along with his exclamation points, question marks and stars which helped guide me through my own initial Bible study three years later when I, too, received Jesus Christ as my Saviour and Lord.

Writing does something for the mind. Simply putting thoughts on paper helps record them in your brain. I love to see people taking notes in church for future reference. I recommend you make notes directly on the pages of your Bible. When that Bible is full, go to another.

You also might want to record your personal *paraphrase* of the passage you're studying. How does it translate into *your* life? A paraphrase is rewriting the Scripture in your own words. You'll be astonished at the results. It will make you study aspects of the verse of which you weren't aware. Also it will help you remember what the passage says.

(3) *Read devotionally.* I recommend you read the Bible seriously, as you would study a book. But in order to get the most out of the Christian life, you should read it devotionally—believing God will give you hidden nuggets of gold as you dip your pan into its stream.

Let me give you an example of this in my life several years ago.

One day I was alone in our little cabin in the Blue Ridge Mountains of North Carolina. It was just a few weeks after my father had died. I had come to the cabin without my wife or children to work my way through my grief. One afternoon, sitting in an old rocking chair on the front porch, looking out at the brilliant autumn colors sprinkled across the mountains, I opened my Bible to the Twenty-third Psalm—an old favorite. I read it through casually, but my eye stopped and rested on verse four: ***"Your rod and Your staff protect and comfort me."***

The property where our mountain cabin is located had been developed by my father over the last 40 years. He had the land cleared, had a stonemason come in and build the rock wall beside the driveway, and had worked with our old friend and neighbor, Raymond Cox, to build up the cabins. He loved this place and would come up during the hot summer months to escape the Florida heat. He also loved to come up in the autumn to sit on this porch, rock in this chair, and enjoy the beautiful colors of nature. Everywhere I looked, I saw my father's signature on the property.

I glanced up from my Bible, blinking back the tears of grief, and saw—standing in the corner of the porch—my father's favorite walking stick. He had carved it out of a crooked rhododendron branch. Although it looked much like an Irish shillelagh, I saw it as something far more. I could still hear my father that day when I was a sophisticated sophomore in college—still far from the Lord. Daddy, who had surrendered his life to Jesus Christ the summer before, had finished carving and sanding the walking stick. Holding it up for me to see, he grinned and said, "From this time on, every time you see this old stick, you will be reminded that it is God's rod and God's staff which bring you comfort."

Suddenly the grief was gone. In its place was the Presence of God.

Read the Bible devotionally, and let God meet you at your place of greatest need—perhaps through a simple verse and a small reminder at your elbow.

(4) *Ask questions.* The Bible is not so sacred that it cannot stand honest examination. Ask *when* a thing took place.

Ask *why* it was included in the Bible. Ask *where* it happened. Ask *who* was writing, *whom* it was written about and to *whom* it was written. Ask *what* it meant at that time and *what* it should mean to you. Don't be frustrated if your study raises more questions than you can answer. You are dipping into a great well of spiritual knowledge that has no limits but will quench all thirst.

(5) *Respond.* Bible study is not an end. It is the means to an end. Many people have studied, even memorized the Bible, but have not responded personally to its call on their lives. The reason we study the Bible is so we can discover God's will for our lives—and apply it. Your study will uncover many things God wants you to do. But unless you respond, all your Bible study will be meaningless.

I once read of a mule standing exactly between two identical haystacks. He was extremely hungry, but the poor animal stood there and starved to death because it never could make up its mind from which stack to eat.

Often we find ourselves in the same position as that mule. We read the Bible and in it we find God's will for our lives. But since that will usually is in conflict with something else going on in our lives—we simply stand still where we are . . . and starve to death.

The Swedish Nightingale, Jenny Lind, whose real name was Goldschmidt, won great success as an opera singer. She was at one time the richest and most famous singer in the world. Then one day, at the height of her fabulous career, she left the stage and never returned—choosing to live in privacy.

One day an English friend found her sitting on the steps of a small beach cottage watching a magnificent sunset over the ocean. On her knees was an open Bible. They talked and eventually the English woman asked the inevitable question. "Madam Goldschmidt, how is it that you came to abandon the stage at the very height of your success?"

The famous singer answered quietly. "When every day it made me think less of this," she said, laying her hand on the Bible, "and nothing at all of that," and she pointed to the sunset, "what else could I do?"

Jenny Lind did more than read her Bible. She responded to its call on her life as well.

(6) *Memorize your Bible.* Nothing will make the Bible part of you as much as memorizing verses. **"I have hidden Your word in my heart,"** the psalmist said, **"that I might not sin against You"** (Psalms 119:11). Remembering that Jesus Christ is the "Word," and it is His presence which keeps us from sinning against God, nevertheless, memorizing Scripture and hiding it in our hearts keeps the Presence of Christ fresh.

Prisoners of war in North Vietnam brought back stories of how they had pieced together all the verses of Scripture they had memorized to form a partial Bible. It was these verses which helped some of them make it through those horrible years of imprisonment.

My mother and father established a pattern of Bible memorization which they carried on for years—committing one verse a week to memory. I know others who memorize a verse a day. Some people choose to memorize entire chapters at a time. A friend keeps Bible verses, written on little cards, above the sun visor of his car. When he is waiting at a traffic light, he flips down the sun visor and works on his Bible memorization. I have another friend, a jungle pilot who flies missionaries over the vast expanses of the Amazon jungle in small airplanes. He studies his Scripture cards as he flies. A famous Bible teacher testifies that memorizing portions of the Bible was the secret to his overcoming an "uncurable" learning disability. Another says memorizing passages from the Bible helped him overcome stuttering.

"Your word is a lamp for my feet and a light for my path," David said (Psalms 119:105). Hide it in your heart and it will bring inner light as well.

(7) *Use Bible helps.* There are a number of good books which will help you study the Bible. Keep in mind that no book about the Bible is as good as the Bible itself, but the use of study aids will make things easier. Here are some books which you will want to get to help you along:

(a) *Concordance.* A concordance is a book that lists all the words of the Bible and all the places that word is used. For instance, let's say you remember there is a verse of Scripture someplace in the Bible that talks about "the dark valley of death." Go to your concordance and look up the word *valley* or the word *death* just as you would look up a word in the dictionary. You will then find several Scripture references after each one. With *valley* you'll find a number of references. The Bible talks about a "valley of dry bones" in Ezekiel 37:1, about a "valley of decision" in Joel 3:14, and about the "lily of the valley" in Song of Songs 2:1. But if you keep checking, you'll find a reference to "the dark valley of death" in Psalms 23:4.

I recommend you start with a simple English concordance such as *Cruden's Complete Concordance* to help you trace words in the Bible.

(b) *Bible Dictionary.* A Bible dictionary is a cross between a dictionary and a one-volume encyclopedia. It is a collection of articles explaining places, people and other subjects of the Bible. One of the best is the *New Bible Dictionary.*

(c) *Commentary.* A commentary is a running explanation of the Bible chapter by chapter (sometimes verse by verse). It explains what the text is about. Commentaries come in many-volumed sets with comprehensive explanations of each verse of Scripture, to the more simple one-volume kinds. A fine one-volume commentary is the *New Bible Commentary.*

(d) *Bible Aids.* There are numbers of books about the Bible. I recommend you visit a good Christian bookstore in your city and ask the clerk to show you around. You'll be amazed at the vast collection of books, Bible atlases, maps and study guides available. They may also recommend to you a good Bible correspondence course which you can enroll in as a more serious Bible student.

A final word is important. While it is good to read the Bible alone in a "quiet time," it is exciting to study it as part of a group. There are thousands of Bible study groups around the nation. Many of these are part of Bible-believing churches. Studying the Bible as a member of a group allows you to have access to what the Holy Spirit is teaching others. It will also help keep you from developing wrong interpretations. Therefore, even though I recommend private Bible study as part of your daily life, I hope you will find a small group of people—either a Bible study group which meets some evening of the week or perhaps a Sunday school class in a nearby church—and begin studying together with others who are also eager to learn more about power for living through Bible study.

Above all, I hope you remember that it is not the Bible but the Author of the Bible with whom you need to have fellowship. It is said that Gainsborough, the artist, longed also to be a musician. He bought musical instruments of many kinds and tried to play them. Once when he heard of a great violinist who brought ravishing music from his instrument, Gainsborough bought the violin on which the master played so beautifully. *Surely,* he thought, *if I have that wonderful instrument, I will be able to play too.* But he soon learned that the music was not in the violin; it was in the violinist.

There is an old story of two men in a large classroom who were called on to recite Psalm 23. One was a published orator trained in speech technique and drama. He repeated the psalm in a powerful way. When he finished, the audience cheered and even asked for an encore that they might hear his wonderful voice again.

Then the other man, who was much older, repeated

the same words—"The Lord is my shepherd; I shall not want." But when he finished, no sound came from the large class. Instead, the people sat in a deep mood of devotion and prayer.

Then the first man, the orator, stood to his feet. "I have a confession to make," he said. "The difference between what you have just heard from my old friend and what you heard from me is this: I know the psalm; my friend knows the Shepherd."

That, my friend, is power for living.

Look straight ahead, and fix your eye
on what lies before you. Mark out a straight
path for your feet; then stick to the path
and stay safe. Don't get sidetracked;
keep your feet from following evil.

Proverbs 4:25-27

SUMMING IT UP

The driveway from my house is dirt. Actually it is a combination of sand and clay we call "marl" in Florida. It winds through the tall pine trees in front of our house and emerges on the country road—which is also marl. However, if you turn left, you will soon hit the pavement. The road continues for a mile and connects with another paved road which in turn takes you out to I-95. Once on I-95 you can drive all the way to the state of Maine on a limited-access, four-lane highway.

If I pull out of my garage and head down my marl driveway, I can honestly say I am on the way to Maine. That does not mean I have arrived at my destination. Nor does it mean I'll get there before anyone else. But though I am still a long way off and far behind, I can still say I am on the way.

If I drive into the ditch which borders the country road in front of my house, and get someone to pull me out, I can still say I am on the way. However, if I stay in the ditch, or if I turn right rather than left when I hit the country road, then I cannot honestly say I'm on the way. Only as long as I'm moving in the right direction am I on the way.

As a Christian you have not arrived at perfection.

There has been only one man who lived the perfect life—only one man who was totally filled with the Holy Spirit. A Christian, however, is one who has determined that the direction of his or her life will be toward Jesus Christ—not away from Him. As long as you have your face toward Jesus, no matter how far behind you are, no matter if your tires are flat, no matter if you stay in the ditch more than on the highway, you are still on the way.

If you've gotten this far in the book, then that is a good indication you're a good piece down the road—and much closer to your destination than when you started. You may not feel any closer. In fact, a lot of things may be going wrong in your life right now. That doesn't make any difference; if you have given your life to Jesus Christ and have allowed the Holy Spirit to fill you, you are heading rightly, no matter how imperceptible the progress.

There are some closing thoughts I want to leave with you. In the first place, the Christian life is not free from temptation. Don't be fooled into thinking that if you were more like Jesus you wouldn't be tempted. Jesus was perfect and was tempted the same way we are.

Also I would like to remind you the Christian life is never free from mistakes. Many of us spend a lot of time in the ditches of life. But as Charles Allen once pointed out, the difference between a sheep and a pig is this: When a sheep falls in a mudhole, it bleats to get out. When a pig falls in, he just lies there and wallows.

As one who has been on the road for a long time, I spend a lot of time pulling over to the side and saying to friends and strangers who are in a ditch, "Though you have fallen, you still can get up and start again."

That's the reason we have a Saviour—to save us from our sin.

A Christian is one who is determined that the way of Christ is the best way and who has fully committed himself to that way.

In the front of my Bible I have penned a reminder to myself. It says simply:

> I cannot turn back, for I have entered into an irrevocable contract with God. I have committed my life to Jesus Christ and He has given me eternal life.

I invite you, if you have not already done so, to join me on the road to God with Jesus Christ. Power for living is yours when you come to Christ. I urge you to do it now.

FOR FURTHER READING

Please Note: The following books can be purchased from your local Christian bookstore or from the publisher. Please do *not* write to *Power for Living* since we cannot supply any of these.

BIBLE VERSIONS

New International Version (NIV)—An authoritative translation written in contemporary English, developed by a team of international world-class Bible scholars. The NIV has been in print for over twenty years and has been widely accepted by Christians. It was developed for public and private reading, teaching, preaching and memorizing use.

New King James Version (NKJV)—This translation continues to retain the beauty and purity of the original King James Version, yet it makes the text more readable. The *MacArthur Study Bible,* a popular edition of the NKJV, offers explanatory notes and study helps by well-known Bible teacher John MacArthur.

New Living Translation (NLT)—A recent and very popular thought-for-thought translation produced by ninety world-class Bible scholars. The NLT is an accurate, easy-to-read translation that is good for study and devotional reading. While utilizing the latest in biblical scholarship, its greatest strength is its warm, emotive style that speaks to the heart in everyday language.

DAILY DEVOTIONAL AIDS

Daily Walk and *Family Walk*—*Daily Walk* will direct you each day to a passage of Scripture to read with a brief overview of the passage's message and an application to present-day circumstances. Also, there is a devotional guide for families called *Family Walk.* These can be ordered by writing to: Walk Thru the Bible Ministries, 4201 North Peachtree Road, Atlanta, GA 30341, or by calling 1-800-868-9300.

Discovery—Reading the Bible every day is one of the best ways to grow in your walk with God. This publication includes thoughtful commentary and study questions that will help you apply the Bible's basic message to your daily life. It can be ordered from Scripture Union, P.O. Box 6720, Wayne, PA 19087, or by calling 1-800-621-LAMP.

BIBLE HELPS

Halley's Bible Handbook—Henry H. Halley. (Grand Rapids, MI: Zondervan Publishing House.) Includes concise Bible commentary, important discoveries in archaeology, related historical data, church history, maps, and more. Indexed.

The Exhaustive Concordance of the Bible—James Strong. (Various publishers.) Every word in the King James Version of the Bible is listed alphabetically with its corresponding verse. Hebrew and Greek dictionaries are included. A tremendous asset in locating forgotten verses.

CHURCH HISTORY

Sketches from Church History—S. M. Houghton. (Carlisle, PA: Banner of Truth Trust, PO Box 621, Carlisle, PA 17013.) A very readable and attractive historical presentation of how the Gospel of Jesus Christ has changed the world and continues to do so today.

CHRISTIAN BELIEF

Beginning Again—D. James Kennedy. (Ft. Lauderdale, FL: CRM Publishing.) This booklet will help the reader to understand better the abundant life of Christ and how to receive His blessings. This can be ordered by calling 1-800-229-9673.

Now That I Believe—Robert A. Cook. (Chicago, IL: Moody Press.) This book is most profitable for young people who want to grow in their Christian faith.

Evidence That Demands a Verdict—Josh McDowell. (Nashville, TN: Thomas Nelson, Inc.) For anyone who wants to overcome doubts about the Bible. This best-seller is one of the most well-known contemporary defenses of the Bible as the inspired Word of God.

CREDITS

Unless otherwise indicated, all Scripture quotations are taken from the *Holy Bible,* New Living Translation, copyright © 1996. Used by permission of Tyndale House Publishers, Inc., Wheaton, Illinois 60189. All rights reserved.

Scriptures marked NCV are taken from the *Holy Bible,* New Century Version, copyright © 1987, 1988, 1991 by Word Publishing, Dallas, Texas 75039. Used by permission.

Appreciation to Josh McDowell for permission to adapt material from his books *Evidence That Demands a Verdict* and *Evidence Growth Guide: Part II* (published by Thomas Nelson, Inc., Nashville, Tennessee).

The Four Spiritual Laws appearing in chapter 3 are printed by permission. © Campus Crusade for Christ, Inc. (1965). All rights reserved.

ILLUSTRATIONS

Page ii *H. Armstrong Roberts.* Courtesy of H. Armstrong Roberts
Page x *Tom Turner.* Courtesy of Turner Direct, Inc., Wayne, NJ
Page 6 By permission of Peter Rodger / CMP, NY
Page 8 By permission of Allsport Photography (USA), Inc.
Page 10 By permission of Liaison Agency, Inc./Alan Weiner
Page 12 By permission of Terry Duggan
Page 14 By permission of Allsport Photography (USA), Inc.
Page 16 By permission of Golf Stock, Inc.
Page 18 By permission of the New York Yankees
Page 20 By permission of Elite International Sports Marketing
Page 22 By permission of The Cooper Aerobics Center
Page 24 Courtesy of U. S. Senate Photo
Page 26 Courtesy of the Arthur S. DeMoss Foundation
Page 30 *Bryan F. Peterson.* Courtesy of The Stock Market
Page 40 *Joseph Van Os.* Courtesy of The Image Bank, New York, NY
Page 46 *Jeff Hunter.* Courtesy of The Image Bank, New York, NY
Page 64 *Donald C. Landerwehrle.* Courtesy of The Image Bank, New York, NY
Page 73 *Jim Whitmer.* Courtesy of Jim Whitmer, Wheaton, IL
Page 77 *Yellow Dog Productions.* Courtesy of The Image Bank, New York, NY
Page 82 *Harald Sund.* Courtesy of The Image Bank, New York, NY
Page 92 *Joseph Devenney.* Courtesy of The Image Bank, New York, NY
Page 95 *John P. Kelly.* Courtesy of The Image Bank, New York, NY
Page 100 *Brett Froomer.* Courtesy of The Image Bank, New York, NY
Page 110 *J. H. Pete Carmichael.* Courtesy of The Image Bank, New York, NY
Page 128 *Gary Cralle.* Courtesy of The Image Bank, New York, NY